THE ULTIMATE RENAL DIET COOKBOOK

Affordable, Quick & Easy Kidney-Friendly Recipes with a 28-Day Meal Plan to Support Kidney Health

Renee R. Legere

Manufactured in the United States of America
Interior and Cover Designer: Danielle Rees
Art Producer: Brooke White
Editor: Aaliyah Lyons
Production Editor: Sienna Adams
Production Manager: Sarah Johnson
Photography: Michael Smith

TABLE OF CONTENTS

TABLE OF CONTENTS

TABLE OF CONTENTS

INTRODUCTION

Last year, during my husband's routine medical check-up, his doctor pointed out some minor but concerning issues with his kidneys and heart. While not immediately life-threatening, these issues were serious enough to prompt a significant change in our lifestyle. On the doctor's advice, we embarked on a journey to improve his health through diet, specifically by adopting a renal diet.

At first, the transition was challenging. We had to rethink our eating habits and learn about new ingredients and recipes that would support kidney health. It was a steep learning curve, but I was determined to make it work for my husband's sake. We gradually replaced our old, unhealthy foods with nutritious, kidney-friendly options.

As we embraced the renal diet, I noticed positive changes not just in my husband's health but in our entire family's well-being. We all began to feel more energetic, and our overall health improved. Cooking became a fun and creative process as I experimented with different flavors and ingredients to keep our meals exciting and satisfying.

The experience was eye-opening. It made me realize how much our diet affects our health and well-being. I felt a strong desire to share what we learned with others facing similar challenges. That's how the idea for this book was born.

In this cookbook, I've compiled a collection of delicious, easy-to-make recipes that are tailored for kidney health. My goal is to make it easier for others to transition to a renal diet and enjoy the benefits of healthy eating. I hope this book will be a helpful resource and inspire others to take control of their health through diet.

DEDICATION

I want to extend my heartfelt gratitude to John, our dedicated family doctor. Your practical advice on diet and health has profoundly impacted our lives. Not only did your guidance help my husband significantly improve his kidney and heart health, but it also made our entire family reconsider and embrace healthy eating habits. Your wisdom and support have been invaluable, and we are incredibly grateful for the positive changes you've inspired in our household. Thank you, John, for your commitment to our well-being and for setting us on a path to better health.

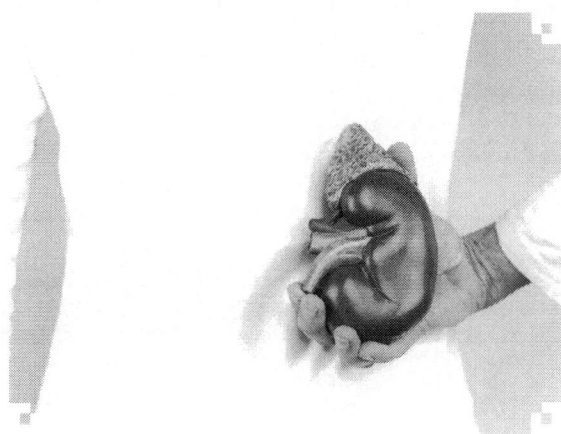

CHAPTER 1: HEALTHY KIDNEYS, HAPPY LIFE

UNDERSTANDING KIDNEY HEALTH

✓ BASIC ANATOMY AND FUNCTION OF KIDNEYS

Our kidneys are incredible organs, each about the size of a fist, located on either side of the spine just below the ribcage. Despite their small size, they perform a massive amount of work to keep our bodies functioning smoothly. The primary job of the kidneys is to filter our blood. Every day, they filter around 50 gallons of blood to remove waste products and excess fluids, which are then excreted as urine. This process is crucial for maintaining the body's fluid balance, electrolytes, and removing toxins.

The kidneys also play a significant role in regulating blood pressure. They do this by controlling the volume of blood (by adjusting the amount of water excreted) and by secreting a hormone called renin, which helps manage blood pressure levels. Additionally, the kidneys produce erythropoietin, a hormone that stimulates the production of red blood cells, and activate vitamin D, which is essential for bone health. It's fascinating to realize that such small organs have such a large impact on our overall health.

✓ COMMON KIDNEY PROBLEMS

Unfortunately, like any part of our body, the kidneys can encounter problems. Some of the most common kidney issues include chronic kidney disease (CKD), kidney stones, and infections.

Chronic kidney disease is a long-term condition where the kidneys do not work as well as they should. It can be caused by various factors, including diabetes, high blood pressure, and certain genetic conditions. CKD often progresses slowly over many years and can eventually lead to kidney failure, requiring dialysis or a kidney transplant.

Kidney stones are another prevalent problem. These are hard deposits made

of minerals and salts that form inside the kidneys. They can be incredibly painful and may cause significant discomfort as they pass through the urinary tract. Factors like dehydration, certain diets, and genetic predisposition can increase the risk of developing kidney stones.

Kidney infections, or pyelonephritis, are typically caused by bacteria traveling from the bladder to the kidneys. Symptoms include fever, back pain, and frequent urination. If not treated promptly, these infections can cause serious damage to the kidneys.

Other issues include acute kidney injury (AKI), where the kidneys suddenly stop working properly, often due to severe dehydration, blood loss, or the use of certain medications. There are also genetic conditions like polycystic kidney disease, where clusters of cysts develop within the kidneys, impairing their function over time.

✓ THE ROLE OF DIET IN KIDNEY HEALTH

Diet plays a crucial role in maintaining kidney health and managing kidney-related issues. What we eat directly affects how hard our kidneys have to work and their overall well-being. Here's a practical guide on how diet impacts kidney health and how we can make better food choices to support our kidneys.

First, let's talk about sodium. High sodium intake can lead to high blood pressure, which is a leading cause of kidney damage. Reducing salt in your diet can help lower blood pressure and decrease the strain on your kidneys. This means cutting back on processed foods, fast food, and salty snacks. Instead, flavor your meals with herbs, spices, and lemon juice, which are delicious alternatives to salt.

Next, consider protein intake. While protein is essential for our bodies, too much of it can be tough on the kidneys, especially for those with existing kidney problems. The kidneys have to work harder to filter out the waste products produced by protein metabolism. Opt for high-quality protein sources like lean meats, eggs, fish, beans, and nuts, and try to balance your intake according to your healthcare provider's advice.

Potassium is another important element to watch. Kidneys help balance the level of potassium in the blood, but when they're not functioning well, potassium can build up to dangerous levels. Foods high in potassium include bananas, oranges, potatoes, tomatoes, and dairy products. If you have kidney issues, your doctor might recommend limiting these foods. Lower-potassium options include apples, berries, carrots, and white rice.

Phosphorus is a mineral that's important for bone health, but too much of it can cause problems for people with kidney disease. The kidneys help regulate phosphorus levels in the body, and when they're not working properly, phosphorus can build up, leading to bone and heart issues. High-phosphorus foods include dairy products, nuts, seeds, beans, and colas. Choosing foods lower in phosphorus, such as fresh fruits and vegetables, rice milk, and light-colored sodas, can be beneficial.

Staying hydrated is also essential for kidney health. Water helps the kidneys remove waste from the blood and maintains the blood vessels' health. While the right amount of water can vary from person to person, a general rule is to drink enough so that your urine is light yellow. However, for those with certain kidney conditions, it's important to follow your doctor's guidance on fluid intake.

Finally, maintaining a healthy weight through a balanced diet and regular exercise can also benefit your kidneys. Obesity increases the risk of developing conditions like diabetes and high blood pressure, which are the leading causes of kidney disease. Eating a variety of fruits, vegetables, whole grains, and lean proteins while limiting sugary foods and drinks can help you achieve and maintain a healthy weight.

GETTING STARTED WITH A RENAL DIET

▶ EXPLANATION OF A RENAL DIET

A renal diet is designed to support kidney health and prevent further damage to the kidneys by controlling the intake of certain nutrients that can be difficult for impaired kidneys to process. When your kidneys aren't working at full capacity, they struggle to filter out waste and excess substances from the blood. A renal diet helps minimize this burden by limiting specific nutrients like sodium, potassium, phosphorus, and protein.

This diet isn't just about cutting things out; it's about making smart choices to ensure you still get the nutrients you need for overall health while protecting your kidneys. It involves eating more of the good stuff—like fresh fruits and vegetables (within limits), lean proteins, and whole grains—while reducing the not-so-good stuff, such as processed foods, salty snacks, and sugary drinks. With the right approach, a renal diet can be both nutritious and delicious.

▶ KEY NUTRIENTS TO MONITOR

Sodium

Sodium is found in salt and is present in many processed and packaged foods. High sodium intake can raise blood pressure and cause fluid retention, putting extra strain on the kidneys. For those on a renal diet, it's crucial to limit sodium intake to help control blood pressure and reduce swelling.

Tips for reducing sodium:

- Avoid adding salt to your food at the table or while cooking.

- Use herbs, spices, and lemon juice for flavor.

- Choose fresh or frozen vegetables instead of canned ones, or rinse canned vegetables to reduce sodium.

- Read food labels carefully and choose low-sodium or no-salt-added options.

Potassium

Potassium is an essential mineral that helps muscles work, including the heart. However, too much potassium can be dangerous for people with kidney issues, as their kidneys may not be able to remove excess potassium effectively. High levels of potassium can lead to serious heart problems.

Tips for managing potassium:

- Be mindful of high-potassium foods like bananas, oranges, potatoes, tomatoes, and dairy products.

- Opt for lower-potassium fruits and vegetables like apples, berries, grapes, carrots, and green beans.

- Boil vegetables and drain the water to reduce their potassium content.

- Check with your healthcare provider for specific recommendations on potassium intake.

Phosphorus

Phosphorus is vital for bone health, but when kidneys are not functioning well, phosphorus can build up in the blood, leading to weakened bones and cardiovascular issues. A renal diet often includes restrictions on high-phosphorus foods.

Tips for limiting phosphorus:

- Avoid foods high in phosphorus such as dairy products, nuts, seeds, beans, and colas.

- Choose foods lower in phosphorus like fresh fruits and vegetables, rice milk, and clear sodas.

- Be cautious with processed foods, as they often contain phosphorus additives.

- Consider phosphorus binders prescribed by your doctor to help control phosphorus levels.

Protein

Protein is necessary for building and repairing tissues, but too much protein can be taxing on the kidneys. The body creates waste products when it breaks down protein, and impaired kidneys may struggle to remove these wastes.

Tips for managing protein intake:

- Focus on high-quality protein sources like lean meats, poultry, fish, eggs, and small amounts of dairy.

- Balance protein intake with other nutrient-rich foods.

- Work with a dietitian to determine the right amount of protein for your individual needs.

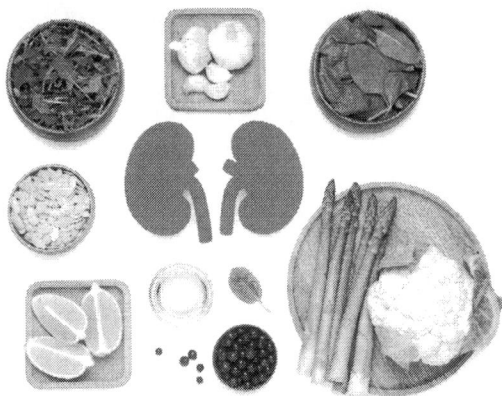

▶ **MEAL PLANNING AND GROCERY SHOPPING**

Starting a renal diet might seem overwhelming at first, but with some planning and smart shopping, it becomes much easier. Here are some practical tips to help you get started:

PLAN YOUR MEALS

- Create a weekly menu: This helps you stay organized and ensures you're getting a balanced diet. Plan meals around renal-friendly recipes and incorporate a variety of foods to keep things interesting.

- Batch cooking: Prepare large quantities of renal-friendly meals and freeze portions for days when you don't feel like cooking. This can save time and reduce the temptation to order takeout.

- Portion control: Use measuring cups and a kitchen scale to ensure you're eating appropriate portions of foods, especially those that need to be limited, like protein and high-potassium foods.

GROCERY SHOPPING TIPS

- Make a list: Based on your meal plan, create a shopping list of the ingredients you need. This can help you avoid impulse purchases that might not be kidney-friendly.

- Shop the perimeter: Most fresh foods, like fruits, vegetables, and meats, are found around the perimeter of the store. Processed and packaged foods, which are often high in sodium, potassium, and phosphorus, are usually in the center aisles.

- Read labels: Look for low-sodium, no-salt-added, and low-phosphorus options. Pay attention to serving sizes to better understand nutrient content.

- Choose fresh or frozen: Fresh or frozen fruits and vegetables are typically lower in sodium and potassium compared to canned options. If you do buy canned, rinse them well to reduce sodium.

COOKING TIPS

- Use herbs and spices: Fresh herbs, garlic, and spices can add flavor without the need for salt.

- Cook from scratch: Preparing meals at home allows you to control the ingredients and avoid hidden sodium and phosphorus additives often found in restaurant or pre-packaged foods.

STAY HYDRATED

While fluid intake recommendations can vary, staying hydrated is generally important. Drink water throughout the day unless otherwise directed by your healthcare provider. Avoid sugary drinks and those high in phosphorus, like colas.

ESSENTIAL INGREDIENTS FOR A RENAL DIET PANTRY

LIST OF MUST-HAVE PANTRY ITEMS

Starting with a well-stocked pantry is key to maintaining a renal diet. Here are some essentials that can help you create a variety of kidney-friendly meals:

LOW-SODIUM BROTHS AND STOCKS:

These can be used as a base for soups, stews, and sauces. They add flavor without the extra sodium.

HERBS AND SPICES:

- Fresh and dried herbs like basil, parsley, thyme, and cilantro.
- Spices such as cumin, turmeric, paprika, and cinnamon.
- Garlic powder and onion powder (but not garlic salt or onion salt).

VINEGARS:

Apple cider vinegar, balsamic vinegar, and red wine vinegar can add zest to salads, marinades, and dressings.

OLIVE OIL AND CANOLA OIL:

These heart-healthy oils are great for cooking and salad dressings.

WHOLE GRAINS:

White rice, bulgur, couscous, and quinoa are excellent staples. Unlike brown rice, these options are lower in potassium and phosphorus.

PASTA AND NOODLES:

Opt for plain pasta and noodles, which are low in sodium and versatile.

CANNED OR DRIED BEANS:

Choose low-sodium varieties and rinse canned beans thoroughly to reduce sodium content.

UNSALTED CRACKERS AND RICE CAKES:

These make for convenient snacks and are low in sodium.

CANNED TUNA OR SALMON:

Look for those packed in water with no added salt.

LOW-SODIUM TOMATO PRODUCTS:

Canned tomatoes, tomato paste, and sauce can be used for cooking but choose the no-salt-added versions.

UNSWEETENED APPLESAUCE:

A great snack and can be used in baking as a substitute for oil or butter.

LOW-SUGAR JAMS AND JELLIES:

Perfect for spreading on toast or rice cakes.

RECOMMENDED FRESH PRODUCE

Fresh fruits and vegetables are a cornerstone of the renal diet. However, some produce needs to be limited due to high potassium content. Here are some renal-friendly options:

FRUITS:

- Apples
- Berries (strawberries, blueberries, raspberries)
- Grapes
- Pineapple
- Peaches
- Plums
- Watermelon (in moderation)

VEGETABLES:

- Bell peppers (red, green, yellow)
- Cabbage
- Cauliflower
- Cucumbers
- Lettuce (romaine, iceberg)
- Onions
- Carrots (in moderation)
- Green beans
- Zucchini

LEAFY GREENS:

- Kale and spinach (in moderation due to potassium content)
- Mustard greens and collard greens (cook and drain to reduce potassium)

HERBS AND AROMATICS:

- Fresh garlic
- Fresh ginger
- Fresh herbs like basil, cilantro, and parsley

LOW-POTASSIUM SQUASH:

- Summer squash
- Spaghetti squash

SUBSTITUTES FOR HIGH-SODIUM AND HIGH-POTASSIUM FOODS

Adjusting recipes to fit a renal diet can be easier with the right substitutes. Here are some swaps to keep your meals delicious and kidney-friendly:

HIGH-SODIUM INGREDIENTS:

- **Salt:** Use salt-free herb blends, lemon juice, or vinegar to enhance flavor without added sodium.
- **Soy Sauce:** Opt for low-sodium soy sauce or coconut aminos.
- **Canned Vegetables:** Choose fresh or frozen alternatives, or rinse canned vegetables to reduce sodium.

- **Processed Meats:** Replace with fresh, unprocessed meats like chicken breast, turkey, or lean cuts of pork and beef.

HIGH-POTASSIUM FOODS:

- **Bananas:** Swap with apples, berries, or grapes.

- **Tomatoes:** Use red bell peppers or make a low-potassium tomato substitute with a mix of roasted red peppers and a small amount of low-sodium tomato sauce.

- **Oranges:** Try apples, pears, or blueberries.

- **Potatoes:** Substitute with rice, pasta, or cauliflower. For mashed potatoes, try mashed cauliflower.

HIGH-PHOSPHORUS FOODS:

- **Dairy Products:** Use rice milk, almond milk, or non-dairy creamers instead of cow's milk. Opt for low-phosphorus cheeses like cream cheese and ricotta.

- **Whole Grains:** Choose white bread, white rice, and refined grains over whole grains.

- **Nuts and Seeds:** Limit intake and choose lower-phosphorus snacks like unsalted popcorn or rice cakes.

HIGH-PROTEIN FOODS:

- **Red Meat:** Limit intake and choose high-quality protein sources like chicken, turkey, fish, and eggs.

- **Dairy:** Opt for smaller portions and choose low-protein alternatives like almond milk or rice milk.

ORGANIZING YOUR RENAL DIET PANTRY

Keeping your pantry organized can make meal preparation easier and help you stick to your renal diet. Here are some practical tips:

LABEL EVERYTHING:

Clearly label all pantry items, especially those in bulk containers, to avoid confusion.

GROUP SIMILAR ITEMS:

Store similar items together. For example, keep all grains in one section, canned goods in another, and spices in their own space.

USE CLEAR CONTAINERS:

Store dry goods like rice, pasta, and beans in clear, airtight containers. This keeps them fresh and allows you to see what you have at a glance.

KEEP A SHOPPING LIST:

Maintain a running list of items you need to replenish. This ensures you always have your essential ingredients on hand.

ROTATE STOCK:

When you buy new items, place them behind older ones to ensure you use up what you have before it expires.

MEAL PREPARATION TIPS

Making renal-friendly meals doesn't have to be complicated. Here are some tips to make your cooking experience smoother:

PREP IN ADVANCE:

Wash and chop vegetables ahead of time. Store them in the fridge for quick access.

BATCH COOKING:

Prepare large batches of soups, stews, and casseroles. Freeze portions for easy, ready-to-eat meals on busy days.

FLAVOR BOOSTERS:

Use homemade broths, infused oils (like garlic or herb oil), and salt-free seasonings to add depth to your dishes.

SIMPLE SWAPS:

Experiment with substitutions to make your favorite recipes renal-friendly. For example, use low-sodium broth instead of regular, or swap high-potassium vegetables for lower ones.

In conclusion, building a renal diet pantry involves stocking up on essential low-sodium, low-potassium, and low-phosphorus items, incorporating fresh produce wisely, and finding suitable substitutes for restricted foods. With thoughtful meal planning and smart grocery shopping, you can create delicious, kidney-friendly meals that support your health and make your dietary journey enjoyable.

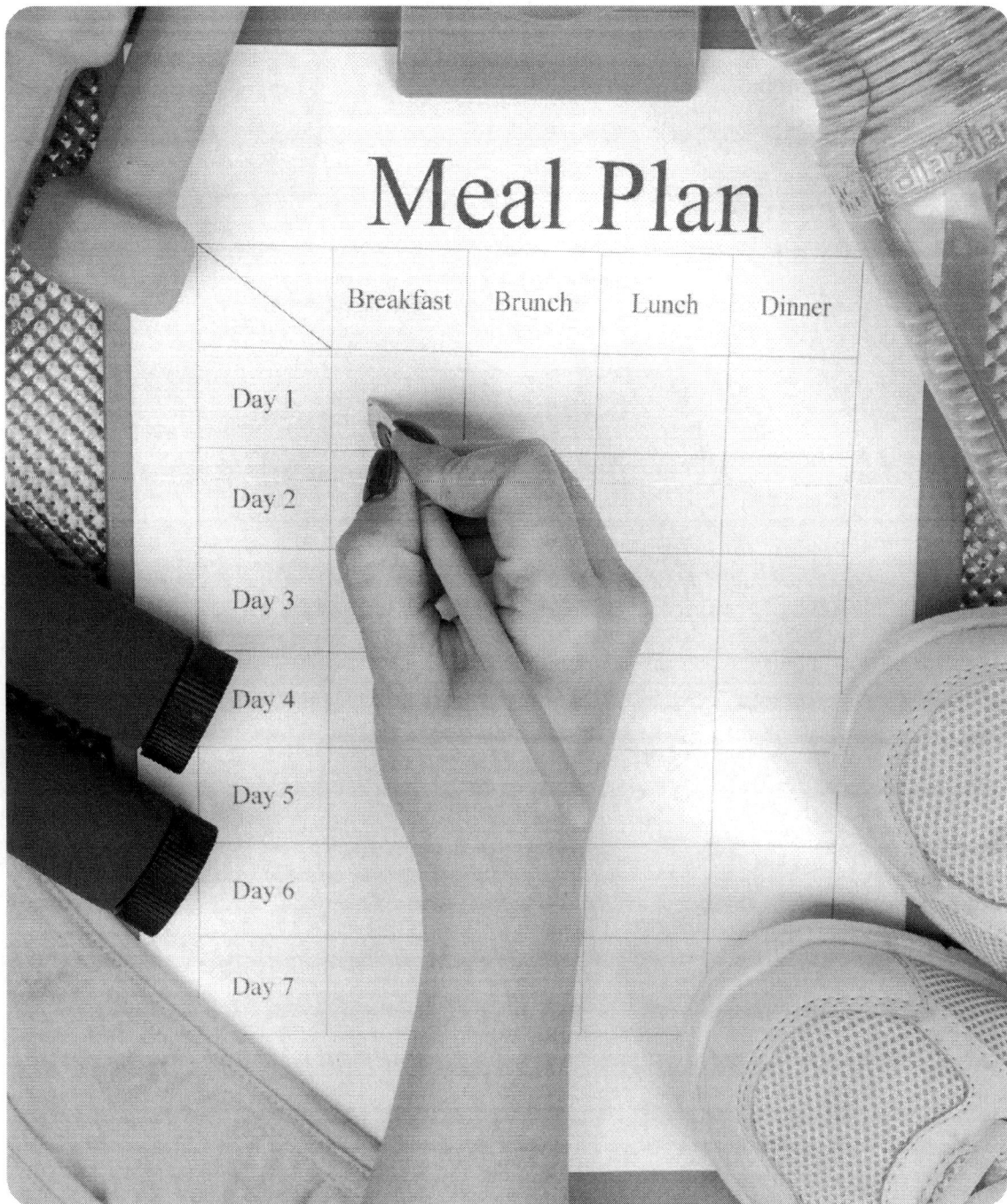

CHAPTER 2: 4-WEEK MEAL PLAN

WEEK 1

Day 1:

Breakfast: **Buckwheat Pancakes**

Lunch: **Roasted Chicken Breast**

Snack: **Toasted Pear Chips**

Dinner: **Lemon Poached Salmon**

Total for the day:

Calories: 966; Fat: 35g; Carbs: 343g; Fiber: 10g; Protein: 67g; Phosphorus: 528mg; Potassium: 1237mg; Sodium: 756.8mg

Day 2:

Breakfast: **Buckwheat Pancakes**

Lunch: **Roasted Chicken Breast**

Snack: **Toasted Pear Chips**

Dinner: **Lemon Poached Salmon**

Total for the day:

Calories: 966; Fat: 35g; Carbs: 343g; Fiber: 10g; Protein: 67g; Phosphorus: 528mg; Potassium: 1237mg; Sodium: 756.8mg

Day 3:

Breakfast: **Kale and Cheddar Frittata**

Lunch: **Roasted Chicken Breast**

Snack: **Toasted Pear Chips**

Dinner: **Lemon Poached Salmon**

Total for the day:

Calories: 1025; Fat: 32g; Carbs: 350g; Fiber: 8g; Protein: 73g; Phosphorus: 464 mg; Potassium: 1039mg; Sodium: 614.9mg

Day 4:

Breakfast: **Kale and Cheddar Frittata**

Lunch: **Lemon Poached Salmon**

Snack: **Toasted Pear Chips**

Dinner: **Roasted Chicken Breast**

Total for the day:

Calories: 1025; Fat: 32g; Carbs: 350g; Fiber: 8g; Protein: 73g; Phosphorus: 464 mg; Potassium: 1039mg; Sodium: 614.9mg

Day 5:

Breakfast: **Kale and Cheddar Frittata**

Lunch: **Barley and Roasted Vegetable Bowl**

Snack: **Fruit Salad**

Dinner: **Roasted Chicken Breast**

Total for the day:

Calories: 1164; Fat: 33.4g; Carbs: 388g; Fiber: 21g; Protein: 71g; Phosphorus: 447 mg; Potassium: 1155mg; Sodium: 771.9 mg

Day 6:

Breakfast: **Buckwheat Pancakes**

Lunch: **Barley and Roasted Vegetable Bowl**

Snack: **Fruit Salad**

Dinner: **Roasted Chicken Breast**

Total for the day:

Calories: 1105; Fat: 36.4g; Carbs: 381g; Fiber: 23g; Protein: 65g; Phosphorus: 511 mg; Potassium: 1353mg; Sodium: 912.9mg

Day 7:

Breakfast: **Buckwheat Pancakes**

Lunch: **Barley and Roasted Vegetable Bowl**

Snack: **Fruit Salad**

Dinner: **Barley and Roasted Vegetable Bowl**

Total for the day:

Calories: 946; Fat: 29.4g; Carbs: 148g; Fiber: 32g; Protein: 32g; Phosphorus: 591 mg; Potassium: 1572mg; Sodium: 549mg

WEEK 2

Day 1:

Breakfast: **Blueberry Baked Bread**

Lunch: **Crispy Fried Chicken**

Snack: **Onion Bagel Chips**

Dinner: **White Fish and Broccoli Curry**

Total for the day:

Calories: 893; Fat: 47g; Carbs: 78g; Fiber: 29g; Protein: 74g; Phosphorus: 684mg; Potassium: 1194mg; Sodium: 689mg

Day 2:

Breakfast: **Blueberry Baked Bread**

Lunch: **Crispy Fried Chicken**

Snack: **Onion Bagel Chips**

Dinner: **White Fish and Broccoli Curry**

Total for the day:

Calories: 893; Fat: 47g; Carbs: 78g; Fiber: 29g; Protein: 74g; Phosphorus: 684mg; Potassium: 1194mg; Sodium: 689mg

Day 3:

Breakfast: **Baked Egg Casserole**

Lunch: **Crispy Fried Chicken**

Snack: **Onion Bagel Chips**

Dinner: **White Fish and Broccoli Curry**

Total for the day:

Calories: 833; Fat: 43g; Carbs: 68g; Fiber: 13g; Protein: 62g; Phosphorus: 706 mg; Potassium: 1189mg; Sodium: 538mg

Day 4:

Breakfast: **Baked Egg Casserole**

Lunch: **Crispy Fried Chicken**

Snack: **Onion Bagel Chips**

Dinner: **Italian Style Meatballs**

Total for the day:

Calories: 769; Fat: 36g; Carbs: 61g; Fiber: 11g; Protein: 65g; Phosphorus: 718 mg; Potassium: 1010mg; Sodium: 547mg

Day 5:

Breakfast: **Baked Egg Casserole**

Lunch: **Italian Style Meatballs**

Snack: **Onion Bagel Chips**

Dinner: **White Fish and Broccoli Curry**

Total for the day:

Calories: 746; Fat: 42g; Carbs: 49g; Fiber: 12g; Protein: 60g; Phosphorus: 694 mg; Potassium: 1239mg; Sodium: 475mg

Day 6:

Breakfast: **Blueberry Baked Bread**

Lunch: **Italian Style Meatballs**

Snack: **Baked Yellow Squash**

Dinner: **White Fish and Broccoli Curry**

Total for the day:

Calories: 767; Fat: 34g; Carbs: 48g; Fiber: 11g; Protein: 72g; Phosphorus: 532 mg; Potassium: 1024mg; Sodium: 578mg

Day 7:

Breakfast: **Blueberry Baked Bread**

Lunch: **Italian Style Meatballs**

Snack: **Baked Yellow Squash**

Dinner: **White Fish and Broccoli Curry**

Total for the day:

Calories: 767; Fat: 34g; Carbs: 48g; Fiber: 11g; Protein: 72g; Phosphorus: 532 mg; Potassium: 1024mg; Sodium: 578mg

WEEK 3

Day 1:

Breakfast: Old-Fashioned Strawberry Bread

Lunch: Spicy Pork Tenderloin

Snack: Mozzarella Cheese Cookies

Dinner: Lime Asparagus Spaghetti

Total for the day:

Calories: 1148; Fat: 56g; Carbs: 194g; Fiber: 11g; Protein: 102.3g; Phosphorus: 525 mg; Potassium: 853mg; Sodium: 606mg

Day 2:

Breakfast: Old-Fashioned Strawberry Bread

Lunch: Spicy Pork Tenderloin

Snack: Mozzarella Cheese Cookies

Dinner: Lime Asparagus Spaghetti

Total for the day:

Calories: 1148; Fat: 56g; Carbs: 194g; Fiber: 11g; Protein: 102.3g; Phosphorus: 525 mg; Potassium: 853mg; Sodium: 606mg

Day 3:

Breakfast: Old-Fashioned Strawberry Bread

Lunch: Spicy Pork Tenderloin

Snack: Mozzarella Cheese Cookies

Dinner: Lime Asparagus Spaghetti

Total for the day:

Calories: 1148; Fat: 56g; Carbs: 194g; Fiber: 11g; Protein: 102.3g; Phosphorus: 525 mg; Potassium: 853mg; Sodium: 606mg

Day 4:

Breakfast: Old-Fashioned Strawberry Bread

Lunch: Spicy Pork Tenderloin

Snack: Mozzarella Cheese Cookies

Dinner: Lime Asparagus Spaghetti

Total for the day:

Calories: 1148; Fat: 56g; Carbs: 194g; Fiber: 11g; Protein: 102.3g; Phosphorus: 525 mg; Potassium: 853mg; Sodium: 606mg

Day 5:

Breakfast: Old-Fashioned Strawberry Bread

Lunch: Lime Asparagus Spaghetti

Snack: Mozzarella Cheese Cookies

Dinner: Tangy Glazed Black Cod

Total for the day:

Calories: 780; Fat: 35g; Carbs: 193.8g; Fiber: 11.2g; Protein: 46.8g; Phosphorus: 313 mg; Potassium: 548mg; Sodium: 519mg

Day 6:

Breakfast: Apple Pie Smoothie

Lunch: Lime Asparagus Spaghetti

Snack: Cinnamon Apple Chia Seed Pudding

Dinner: Tangy Glazed Black Cod

Total for the day:

Calories: 476; Fat: 10g; Carbs: 85.8g; Fiber: 15.2g; Protein: 11.5g; Phosphorus: 341 mg; Potassium: 1088mg; Sodium: 295mg

Day 7:

Breakfast: Apple Pie Smoothie

Lunch: Tangy Glazed Black Cod

Snack: Cinnamon Apple Chia Seed Pudding

Dinner: Tangy Glazed Black Cod

Total for the day:

Calories: 349; Fat: 7g; Carbs: 67.8g; Fiber: 13.2g; Protein: 6g; Phosphorus: 212 mg; Potassium: 586mg; Sodium: 347mg

WEEK 4

Day 1:

Breakfast: **Curried Egg Pita Pockets**

Lunch: **Ground Chicken with Basil**

Snack: **Strawberry Ice Cream**

Dinner: **Barbecue Beef**

Total for the day:

Calories: 1164; Fat: 53.8g; Carbs: 95g; Fiber: 19g; Protein: 71g; Phosphorus: 642 mg; Potassium: 1680.3mg; Sodium: 413.3mg

Day 2:

Breakfast: **Curried Egg Pita Pockets**

Lunch: **Ground Chicken with Basil**

Snack: **Strawberry Ice Cream**

Dinner: **Barbecue Beef**

Total for the day:

Calories: 1164; Fat: 53.8g; Carbs: 95g; Fiber: 19g; Protein: 71g; Phosphorus: 642 mg; Potassium: 1680.3mg; Sodium: 413.3mg

Day 3:

Breakfast: **Curried Egg Pita Pockets**

Lunch: **Ground Chicken with Basil**

Snack: **Strawberry Ice Cream**

Dinner: **Black Bean Burgers**

Total for the day:

Calories: 1046; Fat: 42.8g; Carbs: 103g; Fiber: 25g; Protein: 60g; Phosphorus: 537 mg; Potassium: 1373.3mg; Sodium: 570.3mg

Day 4:

Breakfast: **Curried Egg Pita Pockets**

Lunch: **Ground Chicken with Basil**

Snack: **Strawberry Ice Cream**

Dinner: **Black Bean Burgers**

Total for the day:

Calories: 1046; Fat: 42.8g; Carbs: 103g; Fiber: 25g; Protein: 60g; Phosphorus: 537 mg; Potassium: 1373.3mg; Sodium: 570.3mg

Day 5:

Breakfast: **Cherry Berry Bulgur Bowl**

Lunch: **Black Bean Burgers**

Snack: **Strawberry Ice Cream**

Dinner: **Ground Chicken with Basil**

Total for the day:

Calories: 1158; Fat: 40g; Carbs: 143g; Fiber: 30g; Protein: 62g; Phosphorus: 666 mg; Potassium: 1642.3mg; Sodium: 516.3mg

Day 6:

Breakfast: **Cherry Berry Bulgur Bowl**

Lunch: **Barbecue Beef**

Snack: **Strawberry Ice Cream**

Dinner: **Ground Chicken with Basil**

Total for the day:

Calories: 1278; Fat: 51.8g; Carbs: 109g; Fiber: 22g; Protein: 73g; Phosphorus: 771 mg; Potassium: 1949.3mg; Sodium: 360.3mg

Day 7:

Breakfast: **Cherry Berry Bulgur Bowl**

Lunch: **Barbecue Beef**

Snack: **Strawberry Ice Cream**

Dinner: **Ground Chicken with Basil**

Total for the day:

Calories: 1278; Fat: 51.8g; Carbs: 109g; Fiber: 22g; Protein: 73g; Phosphorus: 771 mg; Potassium: 1949.3mg; Sodium: 360.3mg

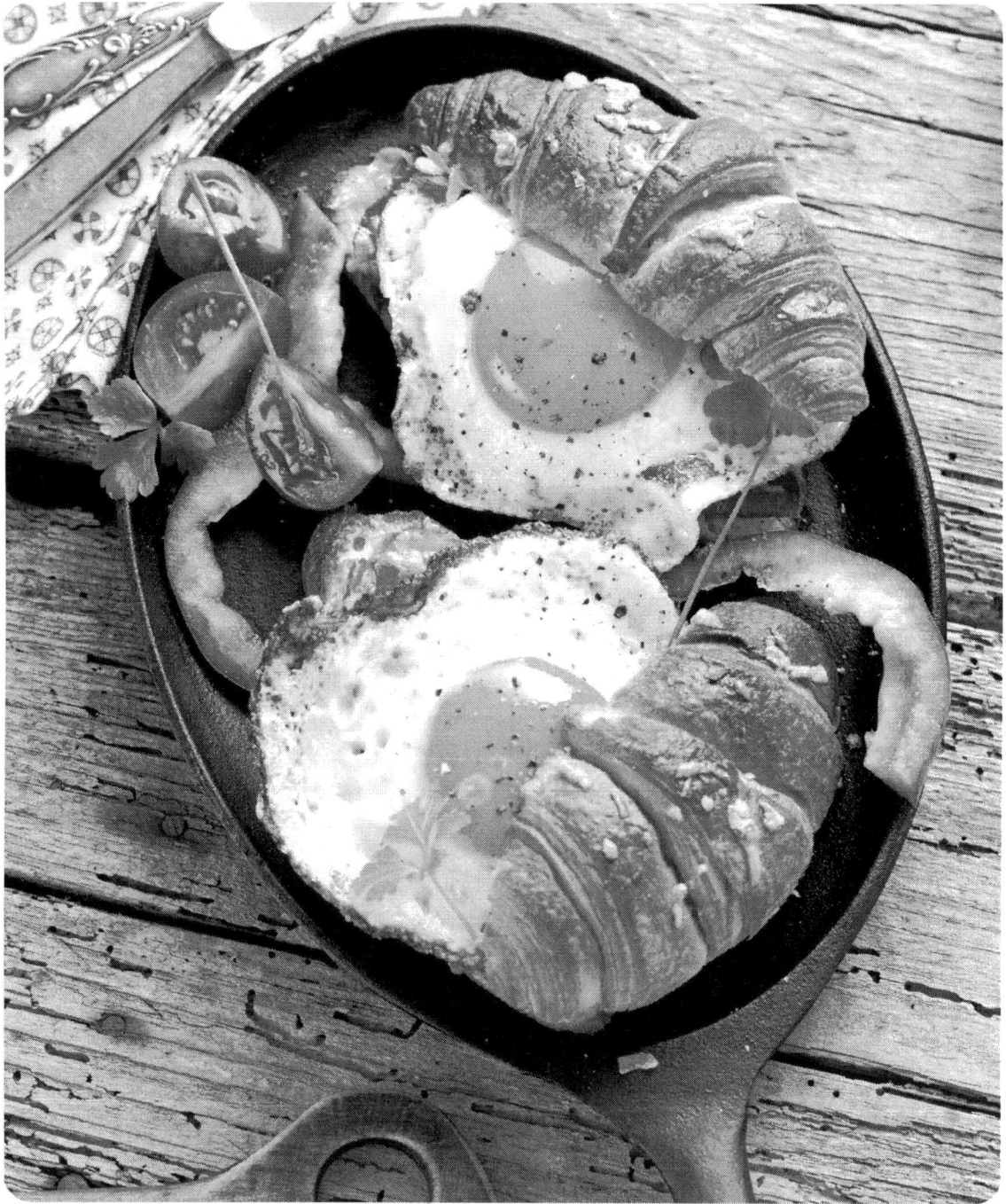

CHAPTER 3:
BREAKFAST

BROCCOLI AND CHEDDAR MINI QUICHES

Prep time: **15 minutes** | Cook time: **35 minutes** | Makes **12 mini quiches**

- nonstick cooking spray
- all-purpose flour, for dusting
- Pie Crust
- 4 large eggs
- ½ cup unsweetened plain almond milk
- 1 tsp freshly ground black pepper
- ½ tsp red pepper flakes
- ½ cup chopped white onion
- ½ cup chopped broccoli florets
- ½ cup shredded aged sharp Cheddar cheese

1. Preheat the oven to 375°F. Coat a muffin tin with nonstick spray.
2. On a lightly floured counter, using your hands or a rolling pin, flatten each dough ball into a round. with a small cookie cutter or the rim of a glass, cut out 12 rounds of dough.
3. Place one round of dough in each well of the prepared muffin tin and bake for 10 minutes.
4. Meanwhile, in a medium bowl, whisk the eggs and milk until light and airy. Add the black pepper, red pepper flakes, onion, broccoli, and cheese and stir to combine.
5. Remove the muffin tin from the oven. Divide the egg mixture evenly among the quiche crusts and bake for 15 to 25 minutes, until the eggs are set.

Per Serving

Calories: **439** | Protein: **11g** | Fat: **17g** | Carbs: **37g** | Fiber: **2g** | Phosphorus: **173mg** | Potassium: **161mg** | Sodium: **127mg**

BUCKWHEAT PANCAKES

Prep time: **10 minutes** | Cook time: **15 minutes** | Serves **4**

- 1¾ cups homemade rice milk or unsweetened store-bought rice milk
- 2 tsp white vinegar
- 1 cup buckwheat flour
- ½ cup all-purpose flour
- 1 tbsp sugar
- 2 tsp Phosphorus-Free Baking Powder
- 1 large egg
- 1 tsp vanilla extract
- 2 tbsp butter, for the skillet

1. In a small bowl, combine the rice milk and vinegar. Let sit for 5 minutes.
2. Meanwhile, in a large bowl, mix the buckwheat flour and all-purpose flour. Add the sugar and baking powder, stirring to blend.
3. Add the egg and vanilla to the rice milk and stir to blend. Add the wet ingredients to the dry, and stir until just mixed.
4. In a large skillet over medium heat, melt 1½ tsp of butter. Use a ¼-cup measuring cup to scoop the batter into the skillet. Cook for 2 to 3 minutes, until small bubbles form on the surface of the pancakes. Flip and cook on the opposite side for 1 to 2 minutes.
5. Transfer the pancakes to a serving platter, and in batches, continue cooking the remaining batter in the skillet, adding more butter as needed.

Per Serving

Calories: **264** | Fat: **9g** | Carbs: **39g** | Fiber: **3g** | Protein: **7g** | Phosphorus: **147mg** | Potassium: **399mg** | Sodium: **232mg**

FRUIT AND CHEESE BREAKFAST WRAP

Prep time: **10 minutes** | Cook time: **30 minutes** | Serves **2**

- 2 (6-inch) flour tortillas
- 2 tbsp plain cream cheese
- 1 apple, peeled, cored, and sliced thin
- 1 tbsp honey

1. Lay both tortillas on a clean work surface and spread 1 tbsp of cream cheese onto each tortilla, leaving about ½ inch around the edges.
2. Arrange the apple slices on the cream cheese, just off the center of the tortilla on the side closest to you, leaving about 1½ inches on each side and 2 inches on the bottom.
3. Drizzle the apples lightly with honey.
4. Fold the left and right edges of the tortillas into the center, laying the edge over the apples.
5. Taking the tortilla edge closest to you, fold it over the fruit and the side pieces. Roll the tortilla away from you, creating a snug wrap.
6. Repeat with the second tortilla.

Per Serving

Calories: **188** | Fat: **6g** | Carbs: **33g** | Phosphorus: **73mg** | Potassium: **136mg** | Sodium: **177mg** | Protein: **4g** | Fiber: **2g**

OLD-FASHIONED STRAWBERRY BREAD

Prep time: **15 minutes** | Cook time: **1 hour and 10 minutes** | Serves **6**

- 3 cup flour
- 2 tsp sugar
- 1 tsp baking soda
- 1 tsp salt (can decrease to ½ tsp)
- 2 tsp oil
- ½ cup apple sauce
- 4 eggs (beaten)
- 20 oz strawberries (frozen or fresh sweetened)
- 1 tsp vanilla

1. Combine sugar, salt, flour and soda (dry ingredients).
2. In the center, make a well.
3. Mix liquids in another bowl (applesauce, strawberries, vanilla and eggs) and place in the well.
4. Combine by hand, keeping the strawberries intact a bit. No need to overmix.
5. Pour into two greased loaf pans.
6. Bake for 1 hour at 350°F.

Per Serving

Calories: **321** | Protein: **24g** | Carbs: **87g** | Fat: **15g** | Fiber: **9g** | Sodium: **112mg** | Potassium: **221mg** | Phosphorus: **136mg**

BLUEBERRY BAKED BREAD

Prep time: **10 minutes** | Cook time: **20 minutes** | Serves **4**

- 1 quart blueberries, fresh or frozen
- ¼ cup water (omit if berries are frozen)
- 1 tsp lemon juice
- ½ cup of sugar
- 1 pinch nutmeg
- 1 pinch cinnamon
- 1 tbsp margarine
- 3 slices bread, buttered and sprinkled with cinnamon and sugar on both sides

1. Preheat the oven to 350°F.
2. Wash the blueberries.
3. Mix all the ingredients, except the bread, in a frying pan. Bring to a simmer.
4. In a shallow baking pan, add the cranberry combination, top with the halved bread.
5. Bake (approximately ten minutes) until golden brown.

Per Serving

Calories: **198** | Protein: **21g** | Carbs: **12g** | Fat: **11g** | Fiber: **6g** | Sodium: **213mg** | Potassium: **145mg** | Phosphorus: **98mg**

CHERRY BERRY BULGUR BOWL

Prep time: **15 minutes** | Cook time: **15 minutes** | Serves **4**

- 1 cup medium-grind bulgur
- 2 cups water
- pinch salt
- 1 cup halved and pitted cherries or 1 cup canned
- cherries, drained
- ½ cup raspberries
- ½ cup blackberries
- 1 tbsp cherry jam
- 2 cups plain whole-milk yogurt

1. In a medium saucepan over medium heat, combine the bulgur, water, and salt. Bring to a boil.
2. Reduce the heat to low and simmer, partially covered, for 12 to 15 minutes or until the bulgur is almost tender. Remove the pan from the heat, cover, and let stand for 5 minutes to finish cooking.
3. While the bulgur is cooking, combine the raspberries and blackberries in a medium bowl. Stir the cherry jam into the fruit.
4. When the bulgur is tender, divide among four bowls. Top each bowl with ½ cup of yogurt and an equal amount of the berry mixture and serve.

Per Serving

Calories: **241** | Fat: **5g** | Sodium: **85mg** | Phosphorus: **237mg** | Potassium: **438mg** | Carbs: **44g** | Fiber: **7g** | Protein: **9g**

APPLE PUMPKIN MUFFINS

Prep time: **15 minutes** | Cook time: **20 minutes** | Makes **12**

- 1 cup all-purpose flour
- 1 cup wheat bran
- 2 tsp Phosphorus Powder
- 1 cup pumpkin purée
- ¼ cup honey
- ¼ cup olive oil
- 1 egg
- 1 tsp vanilla extract
- ½ cup cored diced apple

1. Preheat the oven to 400°F.
2. Line 12 muffin cups with paper liners.
3. In a medium bowl, stir together the flour, wheat bran, and baking powder.
4. In a small bowl, whisk together the pumpkin, honey, olive oil, egg, and vanilla.
5. Stir the pumpkin mixture into the flour mixture until just combined.
6. Stir in the diced apple.
7. Spoon the batter into the prepared muffin cups.
8. Bake for about 20 minutes, or until a toothpick inserted in the center of a muffin comes out clean.

Per Serving

Calories: **125** | Fat: **5g** | Sodium: **8mg** | Carbs: **20g** | Fiber: **3g** | Phosphorus: **120mg** | Potassium: **177mg** | Protein: **2g**

BAKED EGG CASSEROLE

Prep time: **15 minutes** | Cook time: **30 minutes** | Serves **4**

- 1 tsp olive oil, plus more for the baking dish
- ½ sweet onion, chopped
- ½ red bell pepper, chopped
- ½ tsp minced jalapeño pepper
- ½ tsp minced garlic
- 1 cup chopped fresh spinach
- freshly ground black pepper
- 8 eggs, beaten
- 1 tbsp chopped fresh parsley

1. Preheat the oven to 375°F.
2. Lightly coat an 8-by-8-inch baking dish with olive oil.
3. In a large skillet over medium-high heat, heat 1 tsp of olive oil.
4. Sauté the onion, bell pepper, jalapeño pepper, and garlic until softened, about 5 minutes.
5. Add the spinach, and sauté until wilted, about 3 minutes.
6. Season the vegetables with black pepper. Transfer to the prepared baking dish.
7. Pour the eggs over the vegetables, and sprinkle with the parsley.
8. Bake until the eggs are firm, about 20 minutes.
9. Cut into 4 servings and serve.

Per Serving

Calories: **128** | Fat: **7g** | Sodium: **62mg** | Carbs: **2g** | Fiber: **0g** | Phosphorus: **120mg** | Potassium: **140mg** | Protein: **9g**

KALE AND CHEDDAR FRITTATA

Prep time: **10 minutes** | Cook time: **20 minutes** | Serves **4**

- 8 large eggs
- 2 tbsp olive oil
- 4 oz (about ½ bunch) lacinato kale, tough stems removed and cut into ribbons
- ¼ tsp kosher salt
- ¼ tsp ground black pepper
- ¼ tsp red pepper flakes, crushed
- 2 cloves garlic, minced
- 1 oz English cheddar, shredded (or any sharp cheese)

1. Heat the oven to 350°F.
2. Beat the eggs in a small bowl and set them aside.
3. In an oven-safe skillet, heat the oil over medium heat. Add the kale, black pepper, salt and red bell pepper and heat, stirring occasionally, until the kale begins to fall. Stir in the garlic and simmer for 2 more minutes. Remove from the heat.
4. Transfer the beaten eggs to the hot skillet and quickly stir them into the kale. Sprinkle the cheese on top and roast in the oven until the eggs are set, about 10 minutes. Cut into 4 equal portions and serve.

Per Serving

Calories: **323** | Protein: **13g** | Carbs: **46g** | Fat: **6g** | Fiber: **1g** | Sodium: **91mg** | Potassium: **201mg** | Phosphorus: **83mg**

CURRIED EGG PITA POCKETS

Prep time: **15 minutes** | Cook time: **5 minutes** | Serves **4**

- 3 eggs, beaten
- 1 scallion, both green and white parts, finely chopped
- ½ red bell pepper, finely chopped
- 2 tsp unsalted butter
- 1 tsp curry powder
- ½ tsp ground ginger
- 2 tbsp light sour cream
- 2 (4-inch) plain pita bread pockets, halved
- ½ cup julienned English cucumber
- 1 cup roughly chopped watercress

1. In a small bowl, whisk together the eggs, scallion, and red pepper until well blended.

2. In a large nonstick skillet over medium heat, melt the butter.

3. Pour the egg mixture into the skillet and cook for about 3 minutes or until the eggs are just set, swirling the skillet but not stirring. Remove the eggs from the heat; set aside.

4. In a small bowl, stir together the curry powder, ginger, and sour cream until well blended.

5. Evenly divide the curry sauce among the 4 halves of the pita bread, spreading it out on one inside edge.

6. Divide the cucumber and watercress evenly between the halves.

7. Spoon the eggs into the halves, dividing the mixture evenly, to serve.

Per Serving

Calories: **127** | Fat: **7g** | Carbs: **10g** | Fiber: **2g** | Phosphorus: **108mg** | Potassium: **169mg** | Sodium: **139mg** | Protein: **7g**

GREMOLATA SCRAMBLED EGGS

Prep time: **15 minutes** | Cook time: **10 minutes** | Serves **4**

- 1 lemon
- ½ cup chopped flat-leaf parsley
- ⅓ cup chopped fresh basil
- 1 tbsp olive oil
- 4 large eggs
- 4 egg whites
- 2 tbsp unsweetened almond milk
- ⅛ tsp salt
- ⅛ tsp freshly ground black pepper
- 1 tbsp salted butter
- 4 slices whole-wheat toast, for serving

1. To make the gremolata, grate the zest from the lemon, then squeeze the juice, into a small bowl. Add the parsley, basil, and olive oil to the juice. Mix and set aside.

2. In a medium bowl, beat the eggs, egg whites, milk, salt, and pepper until smooth.

3. Heat a medium skillet over medium heat.

4. Add the butter and melt. Add the egg mixture to the skillet and drizzle half of the gremolata over the eggs.

5. Reduce the heat to medium-low and cook, stirring occasionally, until the eggs are scrambled and set, and cooked to 160°F (to kill Salmonella), about 8 to 10 minutes.

6. Drizzle the remaining gremolata over the eggs and serve with toast.

Per Serving

Calories: **250** | Fat: **12g** | Sodium: **388mg** | Phosphorus: **178mg** | Potassium: **288mg** | Carbs: **18g** | Fiber: **3g** | Protein: **15g**

CHOCOLATE COCONUT PANCAKES

Prep time: **15 minutes** | Cook time: **15 minutes** | Serves **4**

- 1 cup whole-wheat flour
- 2 tbsp granulated sugar
- 1 tbsp baking powder
- 1 tbsp unsweetened cocoa powder
- ⅔ cup unsweetened lite canned coconut milk
- ¼ to ½ cup water
- 1 large egg
- 1 tsp avocado oil
- ½ tsp vanilla extract
- avocado or olive oil cooking spray
- 2 tbsp maple syrup
- ¼ cup unsweetened coconut flakes
- 1 tbsp raspberries or strawberries, for topping (optional)
- 1 tsp chocolate chips, for topping (optional)
- powdered sugar, for topping (optional)

1. In a large mixing bowl, mix the flour, sugar, baking powder, and cocoa powder.
2. In a medium mixing bowl, mix together coconut milk, ¼ cup of water, the egg, avocado oil, and vanilla.
3. Pour the wet mixture into the dry mixture and slowly fold together until the batter is wet. Add more water, up to ¼ cup, if needed. Be careful not to overmix.
4. Heat a medium pan or griddle over medium heat. Spray the pan with a little bit of cooking spray.
5. Spoon about 2 tbsp of batter onto the pan to form 4-inch pancakes. Cook for 3 to 5 minutes, and flip when you start to see bubbling. Cook for another 3 minutes. Repeat with the remaining batter.
6. Top each pancake with a drizzle of maple syrup and a sprinkle of coconut flakes and any optional ingredients (if using). Serve immediately and enjoy!
7. Store leftovers in an airtight container or resealable bag in the refrigerator for up to 3 days. If freezing, layer parchment paper between the pancakes. Store in an airtight container or resealable bag in the freezer for up to 3 months. When ready to eat, pop the pancakes into the toaster oven at 300°F for 15 minutes to reheat.

Per Serving

Calories: **246** | Protein: **6.2g** | Carbs: **40g** | Fiber: **5g** | Fat: **9g** | Sodium: **399mg** | Potassium: **195mg** | Phosphorus: **225mg**

CHAPTER 4: DRINKS & SMOOTHIES

RASPBERRY-VANILLA SMOOTHIE

Prep time: **5 minutes** | Cook time : **15 minutes** | Serves **4**

- 1 cup low-fat plain probiotic yogurt
- 1½ cups fresh or frozen raspberries
- ¼ cup chopped kale leaves
- ¼ cup cauliflower florets
- 2 tsp vanilla extract
- 1½ cups water
- ½ cup ice cubes

1. Combine the yogurt, raspberries, kale, cauliflower, vanilla, water, and ice cubes in a blender and blend until smooth.
2. Pour into glasses and serve immediately.

Per Serving

Calories: **71** | Protein: **4g** | Fat: **1g** | Carbs: **11g** | Fiber: **3g** | Phosphorus: **106mg** | Potassium: **241mg** | Sodium: **46mg**

HOT SPICED APPLE JUICE

Prep time: **5 minutes** | Cook time: **30 minutes** | Serves **4**

- ½ tbsp nutmeg
- 12 cloves whole
- 4 broken cinnamon sticks
- ¼ tbsps allspice
- 1-quart apple (unsweetened)

1. Put all the ingredients in a casserole.
2. Bring it to a boil slowly and simmer for 20 minutes.
3. Strain and put in cups to serve.

Per Serving

Calories: **78** | Protein: **4.9g** | Carbs: **19g** | Fat: **3.1g** | Fiber: **5g** | Sodium: **125mg** | Potassium: **76mg** | Phosphorus: **32mg**

RASPBERRY CUCUMBER SMOOTHIE

Prep time: **5 minutes** | Cook time: **5 minutes** | Serves **2**

- 1 c. fresh or frozen raspberries
- ½ c. diced English cucumber
- 1 c. Homemade Rice Milk (or use unsweetened store-bought) or almond milk
- 2 tsp. chia seeds
- 1 tsp. honey
- 3 ice cubes

1. Place the raspberries, cucumber, rice milk, chia seeds, and honey in a blender. Then, blend until smooth.
2. Add the ice cubes. Then, blend until thick and smooth.
3. Pour into two tall glasses. Serve immediately.

Per Serving

Calories: **125** | Fat: **1.1g** | Carbs: **23.5g** | Protein: **6g** | Fiber: **3g** | Sodium: **44mg** | Potassium: **199g** | Phosphorus: **54mg**

KIDNEY NOURISHING SMOOTHIE

Prep time: **5 minutes** | Cook time: **0 minutes** | Serves **2**

- Lime juice, fresh, a good squeeze
- ½ large cucumber (peeled and sliced)
- 1-2 tbsps chia seeds or ground flax
- 1 cup blueberries, fresh/frozen
- 1 cup coconut water (or any nut milk or plain filtered water)
- 1 pinch cinnamon
- Stevia (to taste), optional
- 1 cup ice

1. In a power blender, add all the ingredients and secure the lid.
2. Keep Blending for 60 to 90 seconds or until the desired thickness is reached. Serve and enjoy.

Per Serving

Calories: **169** | Protein: **5g** | Carbs: **20g** | Fat: **8g** | Fiber: **0g** | Sodium: **61mg** | Potassium: **45mg** | Phosphorus: **68mg**

APPLE- CINNAMON DRINK

Prep time: **10 minutes** | Cook time: **20 minutes** | Serves **4**

- 13 fresh apples
- 750ml-1L cold water
- 3-4 tbsp cinnamon
- 1-2 tbsp sugar (brown or caster)

1. Peel, chop and cook 13 fresh apples.
2. Once they were half-cooked, add water leaving for 2 minutes
3. Add a lot of cinnamon (3-4 tbsp, but you can add as much as you please, really) and 1-2 tbsp sugar.
4. Keep cooking for another 5 minutes.
5. Drain and put into the new container back in the pan and bring it to the boil.
6. Add more cinnamon and a bit of water to thin it out a bit.
7. Pour into a cup and enjoy.

Per Serving

Calories: **130** | Fat: **0g** | Carbs: **32g** | Protein: **0g** | Fiber: **3g** | Sodium: **20mg** | Potassium: **0g** | Phosphorus: **0mg**

BLUEBERRY BURST SMOOTHIE

Prep time: **5 minutes** | Cook time: **5 minutes** | Serves **2**

- 1 cup blueberries
- 1 cup chopped collard greens
- 1 cup homemade rice milk or unsweetened store-bought rice milk
- 1 tbsp almond butter
- 3 ice cubes
- In a blender, combine the blueberries, collard greens, milk, almond butter, and ice cubes. Process until smooth, and serve.

Per Serving

Calories: **131** | Fat: **6g** | Carbs: **19g** | Fiber: **3g** | Protein: **3g** | Phosphorus: **51mg** | Potassium: **146mg** | Sodium: **60mg**

APPLE PIE SMOOTHIE

Prep time: **5 minutes** | Cook time: **10 minutes** | Serves **2**

- ½ cup chopped fresh or frozen spinach
- 1 cup water
- 1 tsp vanilla extract
- ½ tsp ground cinnamon
- pinch ground cloves
- 3 ice cubes

1. Place the apples, spinach, water, vanilla, cinnamon, and cloves in a blender, and blend until smooth.
2. Add the ice cubes and blend until thick and smooth.
3. Pour into two tall glasses and serve immediately.

Per Serving

Calories: **95** | Fat: **0g** | Sodium: **8g** | Carbs: **21g** | Fiber: **4g** | Phosphorus: **20mg** | Potassium: **200mg** | Protein: **1g**

HAZELNUT CINNAMON COFFEE

Prep time: **5 minutes** | Cook time: **2 minutes** | Serves **1**

- 1 ½ cups fresh brewed Toasted Hazelnut Blend
- 1 cup half & half
- ¼ cup chocolate syrup
- 2 tbsp hazelnut syrup
- ⅛ tsp ground cinnamon

1. Add hot coffee to a 1-quart saucepan.
2. Steadily add all remaining ingredients, then stir.
3. Cook at medium temperature.
4. Put a sprinkle of cinnamon on top and enjoy.

Per Serving

Calories: **161** | Fat: **7g** | Carbs: **23g** | Protein: **2g** | Fiber: **2g** | Sodium: **34.6mg** | Potassium: **219g** | Phosphorus: **100mg**

MIXED BERRY PROTEIN SMOOTHIE

Prep time: **5 minutes** | Cook time: **0 minutes** | Serves **2**

- 4 oz cold water
- 2 scoops of powder, whey protein
- 2 ice cubes
- 1 tsp crystal light, flavor enhancer drops (liquid, any berry flavor)
- 1 cup mixed berries, fresh or frozen
- ½ cup cream topping, whipped

1. Add ice cubes, frozen berries, water, and crystal light drop in a blender. Blend until mixed properly and slushy.
2. Put protein powder and mix.
3. Put cream topping and mix.

Per Serving

Calories: **182** | Protein: **6g** | Carbs: **20g** | Fat: **8g** | Fiber: **2g** | Sodium: **35mg** | Potassium: **66mg** | Phosphorus: **51mg**

MANGO LASSI SMOOTHIE

Perp time: **5 minutes** | Cook time: **1 minute** | Serves **4**

- ½ cup of plain yogurt
- ½ cup of plain water
- ½ cup of sliced mango
- 1 tbsp of sugar
- ¼ tsp of cardamom
- ¼ tsp cinnamon
- ¼ cup lime juice

1. Pulse all the above ingredients in a blender until smooth (around 1 minute).
2. Pour into tall glasses or mason jars and serve chilled immediately.

Per Serving

Calories: **89.02 kcal** | Carbs: **14.31 g** | Protein: **2.54 g** | Sodium: **30 mg** | Potassium: **185.67 mg** | Phosphorus: **67.88 mg** | Fiber: **0.77 g** | Fat: **2.05 g**

ORANGE FLAVORED COFFEE

Prep time: **10 minutes** | Cook time: **10 minutes** | Serves **2**

- ½ tsp of orange peel (dried)
- ½ Of instant coffee
- 1 of coffee-mate powder
- ¾ cup of sugar

1. Mix the above ingredients in a blender until they become powder.
2. with each serving, place 2 rounded tbsp of coffee mixture in a cup and add (boiling) water.

Per Serving

Calories: **82** | Protein: **4.8g** | Carbs: **12.5g** | Fat: **4.5g** | Fiber: **2g** | Sodium: **132mg** | Potassium: **50mg** | Phosphorus: **56mg**

BLACKBERRY KALE SMOOTHIE

Prep time: **5 minutes** | Cook time: **10 minutes** | Serves **2**

- 1 cup fresh or frozen blackberries
- ½ cup chopped fresh kale, stemmed
- 1 cup Homemade Rice Milk (or use unsweetened store-bought)
- ½ tsp vanilla extract
- ½ tsp honey
- ¼ tsp ground cinnamon
- 3 ice cubes

1. In a blender, put the blackberries, kale, rice milk, vanilla, honey, and cinnamon, and blend until smooth.
2. Add the ice cubes, and blend until thick and smooth.
3. Pour into two tall glasses and serve immediately.

Per Serving

Calories: **118** | Fat: **1g** | Sodium: **55mg** | Carbs: **25g** | Fiber: **4g** | Phosphorus: **25mg** | Potassium: **193mg** | Protein: **2g**

CHAPTER 5: SNACKS AND SIDES

SESAME ASPARAGUS SPEARS

Prep time: 10 minutes | Cook time: 10 minutes | Serves 4

- 1 tbsp low-sodium soy sauce
- 1 tbsp freshly squeezed lemon juice
- 2 garlic cloves, minced
- 1 tsp grated fresh ginger
- 1 tsp brown sugar
- 1 tbsp olive or avocado oil
- 1 pound asparagus, trimmed and cut into 1½-inch pieces
- 1 tsp sesame oil
- 2 tbsp sesame seeds
- 1 tsp freshly ground black pepper
- ½ tsp red pepper flakes (optional)

1. In a small bowl, whisk the soy sauce, lemon juice, garlic, ginger, and brown sugar until the brown sugar has dissolved.
2. In a large pan or skillet, heat the oil over medium-high heat. Add the asparagus and cook for about 3 minutes. Add the sauce mixture to the pan, stir together, and cook until the asparagus is tender but still crisp, about 4 minutes.
3. Remove the asparagus from the pan and divide among 4 plates. Drizzle the sesame oil over the asparagus and sprinkle the sesame seeds, black pepper, and red pepper flakes on top (if using). Serve immediately.
4. Store leftovers in an airtight container in the refrigerator for up to 4 days and in the freezer for up to 3 months.

Per Serving

Calories: **107** | Protein: **4.25g** | Carbs: **8g** | Fiber: **3g** | Fat: **8g** | Cholesterol: **0mg** | Potassium: **312mg** | Phosphorus: **103mg**

ROASTED ONION GARLIC DIP

Prep time: 15 minutes, plus 1 hour to chill | Cook time: 1 hour | Serves 6

- 1 large sweet onion, peeled and cut into eighths
- 8 garlic cloves
- 2 tsp olive oil
- ½ cup light sour cream
- 1 tbsp fresh lemon juice
- 1 tbsp chopped fresh parsley
- 1 tsp chopped fresh thyme
- freshly ground black pepper

1. Preheat the oven to 425°F.
2. In a small bowl, toss the onion and garlic with the olive oil.
3. Transfer the onion and garlic to a piece of aluminum foil and wrap the vegetables loosely in a packet.
4. Place the foil packet on a small baking sheet and place the sheet in the oven.
5. Roast the vegetables for 50 minutes to 1 hour, or until they are very fragrant and golden.
6. Remove the packet from the oven and allow it to cool for 15 minutes.
7. In a medium bowl, stir together the sour cream, lemon juice, parsley, thyme, and black pepper.
8. Open the foil packet carefully and transfer the vegetables to a cutting board.
9. Chop the vegetables and add them to the sour cream mixture. Stir to combine.
10. Cover the dip and chill in the refrigerator for 1 hour before serving.

Per Serving

Calories: **44** | Fat: **3g** | Carbs: **5g** | Fiber: **3g** | Phosphorus: **22mg** | Potassium: **79mg** | Sodium: **10mg** | Protein: **1g**

ROASTED MINT CARROTS

Prep time: **5 minutes** | Cook time: **20 minutes** | Serves **6**

- 1 pound carrots, trimmed
- 1 tbsp extra-virgin olive oil
- freshly ground black pepper
- ¼ cup thinly sliced mint

1. Preheat the oven to 425°F.
2. Arrange the carrots in a single layer on a rimmed baking sheet. Drizzle with the olive oil, and shake the carrots on the sheet to coat. Season with pepper.
3. Roast for 20 minutes, or until tender and browned, stirring twice while cooking. Sprinkle with the mint and serve.

Per Serving

Calories: **51** | Fat: **2g** | Carbs: **7g** | Fiber: **2g** | Protein: **1g** | Phosphorus: **26mg** | Potassium: **242mg** | Sodium: **52mg**

ONION BAGEL CHIPS

Prep time: **10 minutes** | Cook time: **25 minutes** | Serves **6**

- 2 3-½-oz plain bagels
- 2 tbsp margarine, melted
- ½ tsp onion powder

1. Using a knife, slice each bagel in half vertically. Place one bagel half on a flat surface, cut side down, and cut into 8 slices vertically. Repeat the process with the remaining bagels.
2. On a baking sheet, place the slices. Combine the onion powder and margarine, and spread on top of the bagels. Bake for 20 minutes at 325°F or until golden brown and crisp. Remove from pan; cool absolutely. Store in an airtight jar.

Per Serving

Calories: **236** | Protein: **12g** | Carbs: **34g** | Fat: **16g** | Fiber: **10g** | Sodium: **136mg** | Potassium: **298mg** | Phosphorus: **174mg**

ASIAN PEAR SALAD

Prep time: **30 minutes, plus 1 hour to chill** | Cook time: **15 minutes** | Serves **6**

- 2 cups finely shredded green cabbage
- 1 cup finely shredded red cabbage
- 2 scallions, both green and white parts, chopped
- 2 celery stalks, chopped
- 1 asian pear, cored and grated
- ½ red bell pepper, boiled and chopped
- ½ cup chopped cilantro
- ¼ cup olive oil
- juice of 1 lime
- zest of 1 lime
- 1 tsp granulated sugar

1. In a large bowl, toss together the green and red cabbage, scallions, celery, pear, red pepper, and cilantro.
2. In a small bowl, whisk together the olive oil, lime juice, lime zest, and sugar.
3. Add the dressing to the cabbage mixture and toss to combine.
4. Chill for 1 hour in the refrigerator before serving.

Per Serving

Calories: **105** | Fat: **9g** | Carbs: **6g** | Fiber: **2g** | Phosphorus: **17mg** | Potassium: **136mg** | Sodium: **48mg** | Protein: **1g**

TOASTED PEAR CHIPS

Prep time: **15 minutes** | Cook time: **3 to 4 hours** | Serves **4**

- 4 firm pears, cored and cut into ⅛-inch-thick slices
- 2 tsp ground cinnamon
- 1 tbsp sugar

1. Preheat the oven to 200°F.
2. Line a baking sheet with parchment paper and lightly coat with cooking spray.
3. Spread the pear slices on the baking sheet with no overlap.
4. Sprinkle with the cinnamon and sugar.
5. Bake until the chips are dry, 3 to 4 hours. Cool completely.
6. Store in a sealed container for up to 4 days in a cool, dark place.

Per Serving

Calories: **101** | Fat: **0g** | Sodium: **2mg** | Carbs: **27g** | Fiber: **5g** | Phosphorus: **17mg** | Potassium: **183mg** | Protein: **1g**

FRUIT SALAD

Prep time: **15 minutes** | Cook time: **0 minutes** | Serves **4**

- 2 cups drained canned fruit cocktail
- 1 cup drained canned pineapple chunks
- 1 cup (hulled) whole or sliced strawberries
- 1 cup peeled apple, cored and diced
- 1 cup marshmallows
- ½ cup whipped topping (non-dairy)

1. Mix all the fruits.
2. Add whipped topping and marshmallows; mix well.
3. Serve chilled and refrigerated.

Per Serving

Calories: **98** | Protein: **7g** | Carbs: **21g** | Fat: **0.4g** | Fiber: **7g** | Sodium: **79mg** | Potassium: **87mg** | Phosphorus: **42mg**

THYME AND PINEAPPLE CRISP

Prep time: **15 minutes** | Cook time: **10 minutes** | Serves **6**

- 1 (20-ounce) can pineapple tidbits in juice, drained, reserving ⅓ cup juice
- ¼ cup brown sugar, divided
- 1 tbsp cornstarch
- ½ tsp dried thyme leaves
- 3 tbsp unsalted butter
- 1¼ cups quick-cooking oats
- ⅓ cup whole-wheat flour
- pinch salt
- 2 tbsp chopped walnuts

1. Stir together the drained pineapple, reserved pineapple juice, 1 tbsp brown sugar, cornstarch, and the thyme leaves in a medium saucepan over medium heat.
2. Cook for 8 to 10 minutes, stirring occasionally, until the mixture is thickened.
3. Meanwhile, combine the remaining 3 tbsp brown sugar and butter in a medium skillet over medium heat, stirring frequently, until the mixture melts.
4. Add the oats, flour, salt, and walnuts to the brown sugar mixture in the skillet.
5. Cook, stirring frequently, until the mixture is a deep golden brown, about 5 minutes. Transfer the oat mixture to a plate.
6. When the pineapple mixture is thickened, top with the oatmeal mixture right in the saucepan and serve.

Per Serving

Calories: **238** | Fat: **9g** | Sodium: **31mg** | Potassium: **221mg** | Phosphorus: **109mg** | Carbs: **39g** | Fiber: **3g** | Protein: **4g**

MOZZARELLA CHEESE COOKIES

Prep time: **5 minutes** | Cook time: **20 minutes** | Serves **6**

- 1 cup softened butter or margarine
- 1 3-ounce softened package mozzarella cheese
- 1 tsp vanilla extract
- Candied cherry halves
- 1 egg yolk
- 1 cup of sugar
- 2 ½ cups all-purpose flour

1. Preheat the oven to 325 ° F
2. Cream butter and mozzarella cheese; slowly add sugar and beat until fluffy.
3. Beat in the egg yolk; add the vanilla and flour and mix well.
4. Chill the dough for at least one hour
5. Form dough into 1-inch balls; place greased cookies on sheets.
6. Gently push one half of the cherry into each cookie.
7. Bake for 12-15 minutes.

Per Serving

Calories: **288** | Protein: **16.3g** | Carbs: **76g** | Fat: **17g** | Fiber: **0g** | Sodium: **213mg** | Potassium: **87mg** | Phosphorus: **68mg**

CREAMY CARROT HUMMUS DIP

Prep time: **15 minutes** | Cook time: **20 minutes** | Serves **6**

- ½ cup canned no-salt-added or low-sodium chickpeas, rinsed and drained
- ½ (14.5-ounce) can low-sodium carrots, rinsed and drained
- 2 garlic cloves, minced
- 3 tbsp tahini
- juice of 1 lemon
- 2 tbsp water
- ¼ tsp ground cumin
- 2 tbsp olive oil

1. Combine the chickpeas, carrots, garlic, tahini, lemon juice, water, and cumin in a blender or food processor and blend until very smooth.
2. Place the hummus in a serving bowl and drizzle with the olive oil. Serve with crackers or raw vegetables, such as cucumbers, for dipping.
3. Store the hummus for up to 3 days in the refrigerator.

Per Serving

Calories: **116** | Fat: **9g** | Sodium: **24mg** | Phosphorus: **77mg** | Potassium: **122mg** | Carbs: **7g** | Fiber: **2g** | Protein: **3g**

BAKED YELLOW SQUASH

Prep time: **5 minutes** | Cook time: **35 minutes** | Serves **2**

- 2 tbsp margarine or butter, melted
- ¾ tsp thyme
- ⅛ tsp black pepper
- 2 cans yellow squash, sliced
- 1 medium onion, chopped
- 1 small stalk celery, chopped
- 1 large bell pepper, chopped
- 1 tbsp lemon juice

1. Preheat the oven to 300°F.
2. Sauté all the ingredients in the margarine, except the lemon juice. Cook until the onions become translucent.
3. Add the juice of one lemon.
4. In a casserole dish, place the sautéed combination.
5. Bake for thirty minutes. Serve hot.

Per Serving

Calories: **187** | Protein: **12g** | Carbs: **23g** | Fat: **4g** | Fiber: **3g** | Sodium: **88mg** | Potassium: **78mg** | Phosphorus: **34mg**

CHAPTER 6:
POULTRY

SWEET CHILI CHICKEN

Prep time: **10 minutes** | Cook time: **15 minutes** | Serves **4**

- 1 tbsp olive oil
- 2 garlic cloves, minced
- 1 cup broccoli florets
- 1 red bell pepper, sliced
- 1 small white onion, sliced
- 5 ounces boneless, skinless chicken thighs, cut into cubes
- ¼ cup Sweet Chili Sauce
- 2 tbsp low-sodium soy sauce

1. In a medium skillet, heat the oil over medium heat. Add the garlic, broccoli, bell pepper, and onion and cook, stirring, until the vegetables are soft, about 5 minutes. Remove the vegetables from the skillet and set aside.
2. In the same skillet, cook the chicken until cooked through and no longer pink inside, about 10 minutes.
3. Add the sweet chili sauce and soy sauce and stir to coat the chicken well. Return the vegetables to the skillet and toss to combine.

Per Serving

Calories: **120** | Protein: **9g** | Fat: **5g** | Carbs: **9g** | Fiber: **3g** | Phosphorus: **115mg** | Potassium: **339mg** | Sodium: **487mg**

CRISPY FRIED CHICKEN

Prep time: **15 minutes** | Cook time: **30 minutes** | Serves **4**

- ½ cup all-purpose flour
- 2 eggs, beaten
- ½ cup Italian seasoned bread crumbs
- ¼ tsp smoked paprika
- 12 ounces boneless skinless chicken thighs
- pinch freshly ground pepper
- olive oil cooking spray

1. Preheat the oven to 350°F.
2. Place the flour on a plate, the eggs in a shallow bowl, and the bread crumbs and paprika on another plate. Line the three dishes in a row.
3. Season a piece of chicken with pepper, and dredge it first in the flour, then the egg, then the bread crumbs until the chicken is completely coated. Repeat for the remaining chicken.
4. Arrange the chicken on a baking sheet, and coat lightly with cooking spray.
5. Bake until the chicken is cooked through, browned, and crispy, about 30 minutes.
6. Serve hot.

Per Serving

Calories: **246** | Fat: **7g** | Sodium: **206mg** | Carbs: **22g** | Fiber: **1g** | Phosphorus: **218mg** | Potassium: **261mg** | Protein: **23g**

BALSAMIC-GLAZED TURKEY WINGS

Prep time: **15 minutes** | Cook time: **7 to 8 hours** | Serves **4**

- 1¼ cups balsamic vinegar
- 2 tbsp raw honey
- 1 tsp garlic powder
- 2 pounds turkey wings

1. In a bowl, put together the vinegar, honey, and garlic powder then mix.
2. Put the wings in the bottom of the slow cooker, and pour the vinegar sauce on top.
3. Cover the cooker and set to low. Cook for 7 to 8 hours.
4. Baste the wings with the sauce from the bottom of the slow cooker and serve.

Per Serving

Calories: **501** | Fat: **25g** | Sugar: **9g** | Fiber: **0g** | Protein: **47g** | Sodium: **162mg** | Potassium: **54mg** | Sodium: **97mg**

ROASTED CHICKEN BREAST

Prep time: **15 minutes** | Cook time: **40 minutes** | Serves **6**

- ½ of a small apple, peeled, cored, and chopped
- 1 bunch scallion, trimmed and chopped roughly
- 8 fresh ginger slices, chopped
- 2 garlic cloves, chopped
- 3 tbsp essential olive oil
- 12 tsp sesame oil, toasted
- 3 tbsp using apple cider vinegar
- 1 tbsp fish sauce
- 1 tbsp coconut aminos
- Salt
- Ground black pepper
- 4-pounds chicken thighs

1. Pulse all the fixing except chicken thighs in a blender. Transfer a combination and chicken right into a large Ziploc bag and seal it.
2. Shake the bag to marinade well. Refrigerate to marinate for about 12 hours. Warm oven to 400 °F. arranges a rack in foil paper-lined baking sheet.
3. Place the chicken thighs on the rack, skin-side down. Roast for about 40 minutes, flipping once within the middle way.

Per Serving

Calories: **451** | Fat: **17g** | Carbs: **277g** | Fiber: **2g** | Protein: **42g** | Phosphorus: **121 mg** | Potassium: **324 mg** | Sodium: **482.9 mg**

SMOKEY TURKEY CHILI

Prep time: **5 minutes** | Cook time: **45 minutes** | Serves **8**

- 12-ounce lean ground turkey
- ½ red onion, chopped
- 2 cloves garlic, crushed and chopped
- ½ tsp of smoked paprika
- ½ tsp of chili
- powder
- ½ tsp of dried thyme
- ¼ cup reduced-sodium beef stock
- ½ cup of water
- 1½ cups baby green lettuce leaves, washed
- 3 wheat tortillas

1. Brown the ground beef in a dry skillet over medium-high heat.
2. Add in the red onion and garlic.
3. Sauté the onion until it goes clear.
4. Transfer the contents of the skillet to the slow cooker.
5. Add the remaining ingredients and simmer on low for 30–45 minutes.
6. Stir through the green lettuce for the last few minutes to wilt.
7. Slice tortillas and gently toast under the broiler until slightly crispy.
8. Serve on top of the turkey chili.

Per Serving

Calories: **93.5g** | Protein: **8g** | Carbs: **3g** | Fat: **5.5g** | Sodium: **84.5mg** | Potassium: **142.5mg** | Phosphorus: **92.5mg** | Fiber: **0.5g**

JALAPENO PEPPER CHICKEN

Prep time: **5 minutes** | Cook time: **35 minutes** | Serves **2**

- 2 tsp jalapeño peppers, finely seeded and chopped
- Vegetable oil 3 tbsps
- Black pepper ¼ tbsp
- 2 to 3 lbs chicken (skin and fat removed)
- Ground nutmeg½ tbsp
- 1 onion, sliced into rings
- Low-sodium chicken bouillon one and a half cups

1. Heat the oil, brown the chicken pieces and set them aside to keep them warm.
2. To the oil and sauté, add the rings of onion. Include the bouillon and bring it, often stirring, to a boil.
3. Give the chicken back to the pan; add the nutmeg and black pepper. For 35 minutes or until the chicken is tender, simmer and cover.
4. For a minute or so, stir in the jalapeño peppers and simmer.

Per Serving

Calories: **288** | Protein: **31g** | Carbs: **23g** | Fat: **11g** | Fiber: **4g** | Sodium: **135mg** | Potassium: **435mg** | Phosphorus: **198mg**

SLOW COOKER CHICKEN FAJITAS

Prep time: **15 minutes** | Cook time: **7 to 8 hours** | Serves **4**

- 1 (14.5-ounce) can diced bell pepper
- 1 (4-ounce) can Hatch green chiles
- 1½ tsp garlic powder
- 2 tsp chili powder
- 1½ tsp ground cumin
- 1 tsp paprika
- 1 tsp sea salt
- Juice of 1 lime
- Pinch cayenne pepper
- Freshly ground black pepper
- 1 red bell pepper, seeded and sliced
- 1 green bell pepper, seeded and sliced
- 1 yellow bell pepper, seeded and sliced
- 1 large onion, sliced
- 2 pounds boneless, skinless chicken breast

1. In a medium bowl, put together the diced bell pepper, chiles, garlic powder, chili powder, cumin, paprika, salt, lime juice, and cayenne, and season with black pepper then mix. Pour half the diced tomato mixture into the bottom of your slow cooker.
2. Layer half the red, green, and yellow bell peppers and half the onion over the bell pepper in the cooker.
3. Place the chicken on top of the peppers and onions.
4. Cover the chicken with the remaining red, green, and yellow bell peppers and onions. Pour the remaining tomato mixture on top.
5. Cover the cooker and set to low. Cook for around 7 to 8 hours, or until the internal temperature of the chicken reaches 165°F on a meat thermometer and the juices run clear, and serve.

Per Serving

Calories: **310** | Fat: **5g** | Carbs: **19g** | Fiber: **4g** | Protein: **46g** | Sodium: **1,541mg** | Protein: **65g** | Phosphorus: **22mg**

CHICKEN SATAY WITH PEANUT SAUCE

Prep time: **10 minutes, plus 2 hours to marinate** | Cook time: **10 minutes** | Serves **6**

For The Chicken:

- ½ cup plain, unsweetened yogurt
- 2 garlic cloves, minced
- 1-inch piece ginger, minced
- 2 tsp curry powder
- 1 pound boneless, skinless chicken breast, cut into strips
- 1 tsp canola oil

For The Peanut Sauce:

- ¾ cup smooth unsalted peanut butter
- 1 tsp soy sauce
- 1 tbsp brown sugar
- juice of 2 limes
- ½ tsp red chili
- flakes
- ¼ cup hot water
- fresh cilantro leaves, chopped, for garnish
- lime wedges, for garnish

To Make The Chicken:

1. In a small bowl, add the yogurt, garlic, ginger, and curry powder. Stir to mix. Add the chicken strips to the marinade. Cover and refrigerate for 2 hours.
2. Thread the chicken pieces onto skewers.
3. Brush a grill pan with the oil, and heat on medium-high. Cook the chicken skewers on each side for 3 to 5 minutes, until cooked through.

To Make The Peanut Sauce:

1. In a food processor, combine the peanut butter, soy sauce, brown sugar, lime juice, red chili flakes, and hot water. Process until smooth.
2. Transfer to a bowl, and sprinkle with the cilantro. Serve with the chicken satay along with lime wedges for squeezing over the skewers.

Per Serving

Calories: **286** | Fat: **18g** | | Carbs: **10g** | Fiber: **3g** | Protein: **25g** | Phosphorus: **33mg** | Potassium: **66mg** | Sodium: **201mg**

GROUND CHICKEN WITH BASIL

Prep time: **15 minutes** | Cook time: **16 minutes** | Serves **8**

- 2 pounds lean ground chicken
- 3 tbsp coconut oil, divided
- 1 zucchini, chopped
- 1 red bell pepper, seeded and chopped
- ½ of green bell pepper, seeded and chopped
- 4 garlic cloves, minced
- 1 (1-inch) piece fresh ginger, minced
- 1 (1-inch) piece fresh turmeric, minced
- 1 fresh red chili, sliced thinly
- 1 tbsp organic honey
- 1 tbsp coconut aminos
- 1½ tbsp fish sauce
- ½ cup fresh basil, chopped
- Salt
- ground black pepper
- 1 tbsp fresh lime juice

1. Heat a large skillet on medium-high heat. Add ground beef and cook for approximately 5 minutes or till browned completely.
2. Transfer the beef to a bowl. In a similar pan, melt 1 tbsp of coconut oil on medium-high heat. Add zucchini and bell peppers and stir fry for around 3-4 minutes.
3. Transfer the vegetables inside the bowl with chicken. In precisely the same pan, melt remaining coconut oil on medium heat. Add garlic, ginger, turmeric, and red chili and sauté for approximately 1-2 minutes.
4. Add chicken mixture, honey, and coconut aminos and increase the heat to high. Cook within 4-5 minutes or till sauce is nearly reduced. Stir in remaining ingredients and take off from the heat.

Per Serving

Calories: **407** | Fat: **7g** | Carbs: **20g** | Fiber: **13g** | Protein: **36g** | Phosphorus: **149 mg** | Potassium: **706.3 mg** | Sodium: **21.3 mg**

SWEET SOY CHICKEN STIR-FRY

Prep time: **10 minutes** | Cook time: **20 minutes** | Serves **4**

- ⅓ cup brown rice or 1 cup cooked brown rice
- 1 tbsp coconut aminos
- 1 tbsp red pepper flakes
- 2 tsp honey
- 2 tsp rice wine vinegar
- 1 tsp cornstarch, dissolved in 2 tsp water
- 2 garlic cloves, minced
- 4 ounces boneless, skinless chicken breast, cut into ½-inch cubes
- 1 tbsp sesame oil, divided
- 6 cups frozen stir-fry vegetable mix

1. Cook the brown rice according to the package instructions and set aside.
2. In a medium bowl, whisk the coconut aminos, red pepper flakes, honey, vinegar, cornstarch mixture, and garlic. Add the chicken and mix together until well coated.
3. In a large wok or pan, heat ½ tbsp of sesame oil over medium-high heat. Add the chicken and cook for 5 to 7 minutes, until browned and heated through.
4. Add the remaining ½ tbsp of sesame oil and the vegetable mix. Cook for 5 to 7 minutes, until warmed through but still firm. You can cook the vegetables for longer if you prefer them softer.
5. Portion out ½ cup of brown rice and ½ of the chicken and veggie mixture. Serve immediately.
6. Store leftovers in an airtight container in the refrigerator for up to 3 days or in the freezer for up to 3 months.

Per Serving

Calories: **362** | Protein: **18.8g** | Carbs: **54g** | Fiber: **8g** | Fat: **9g** | Sodium: **267mg** | Potassium: **291mg** | Phosphorus: **217mg**

MEXICAN-STYLE CHICKEN SALAD

Prep time: 20 minutes | Cook time: 8 minutes | Serves 6

- 4 tbsp olive oil, divided
- 12 ounces boneless skinless chicken thighs, cubed
- 3 tsp chili powder, divided
- ⅛ tsp cayenne pepper
- 2 tbsp freshly squeezed lime juice
- 3 cups butter
- lettuce
- 1 red bell pepper, chopped
- 1½ cups frozen corn, thawed and drained
- 1 jalapeño pepper, minced
- 1 cup crushed yellow tortilla chips
- ½ cup powerhouse salsa

1. Heat two tbsp of oil in a medium skillet over medium heat.
2. Sprinkle the chicken thighs with 1 tsp chili powder and the cayenne pepper and cook, stirring frequently, for 6 to 8 minutes or until the chicken registers 165°F internal temperature.
3. Transfer the chicken to a serving bowl and add the remaining olive oil, remaining chili powder, and the lime juice. Toss to combine.
4. Add the butter lettuce, bell pepper, corn, and jalapeño pepper and toss.
5. Top with the tortilla chips and the salsa and serve

Per Serving

Calories: **270** | Fat: **15g** | Sodium: **161mg** | Potassium: **489mg** | Phosphorus: **186mg** | Carbs: **22g** | Fiber: **4g** | Protein: **14g**

VEGETABLE AND TURKEY KEBABS

Prep time: 20 minutes | Cook time: 10 minutes | Serves 4

- 2 tbsp olive oil
- 2 tbsp freshly squeezed lemon juice
- 2 tbsp yellow mustard
- 1 garlic clove, minced
- 1 tsp dried italian seasoning
- 1 pound turkey tenderloin, cubed
- 16 whole small mushrooms
- 2 red bell peppers, cut into 1-inch pieces

1. Prepare and preheat the grill to medium coals and arrange the rack 6 inches from the heat.
2. In a small bowl, whisk together the olive oil, lemon juice, mustard, garlic, and Italian seasoning. Set aside.
3. Thread the turkey, mushrooms, and bell pepper onto 4 (10-inch) metal skewers, alternating meat and vegetables.
4. Place the kebabs on the rack and brush them with some of the olive oil mixture.
5. Close the grill and cook until the turkey reaches 165°F internal temperature, brushing twice with the olive oil mixture and turning the kebabs occasionally.
6. Brush the kebabs with all of the remaining marinade and cook, turning frequently, for 2 minutes longer. Serve.

Per Serving

Calories: **225** | Fat: **9g** | Sodium: **218mg** | Potassium: **557mg** | Phosphorus: **288mg** | Carbs: **7g** | Fiber: **2g** | Protein: **29g**

CHAPTER 7: BEEF, LAMB AND PORK

BEEF SHISH KEBABS WITH GRILLED CORN

Prep time: **20 minutes, plus 1 hour to marinate** | Cook time: **10 minutes** | Serves 6

- ½ cup apple cider vinegar
- ½ cup olive or avocado oil
- ½ tsp freshly ground black pepper
- ½ tsp dried oregano
- ¼ tsp garlic powder
- 1 pound beef sirloin, cut into 1½-inch cubes
- 2 medium white onions, quartered
- 2 medium green bell peppers, cut into 1½-inch squares
- 1 medium red bell pepper, cut into 1½-inch squares
- 6 medium corn cobs, husks and silks removed

1. In a large bowl, combine the vinegar, olive oil, black pepper, oregano, and garlic powder.
2. Add the sirloin, onions, and bell peppers to the bowl and mix to evenly coat. Cover the bowl with plastic wrap, put in the refrigerator, and let marinate for 1 hour. If using wooden skewers, soak them in water for 30 minutes.
3. Load the skewers with the meat and chopped vegetables, alternating pieces of the sirloin, bell peppers, and corn. Grill the kebabs and corn over medium heat. Cook the kebabs for 4 to 5 minutes on each side. Cooking times can be adjusted based on how well you like the meat cooked. Cook the corn for about 10 minutes, turning often. Serve immediately.
4. Leftovers can be stored in the refrigerator in airtight containers for up to 5 days.

Per Serving

Calories: **381** | Protein: **21.3g** | Carbs: **28g** | Fiber: **4g** | Fat: **22g** | Sodium: **42mg** | Potassium: **586mg** | Phosphorus: **253mg**

CLASSIC POT ROAST

Prep time: **10 minutes** | Cook time: **5 hours** | Serves **8**

- 1 pound boneless beef chuck or rump roast
- ½ tsp freshly ground black pepper
- 1 tbsp olive oil
- ½ small sweet onion, chopped
- 2 tsp minced garlic
- 1 tsp dried thyme
- 1 cup plus 3 tbsp water
- 2 tbsp cornstarch

1. Place a large stockpot over medium heat.
2. Season the roast with pepper.
3. Add the oil to the stockpot and brown the meat all over.
4. Remove the meat to a plate; set aside.
5. Sauté the onion and garlic in the stockpot for about 3 minutes or until they are softened.
6. Return the beef to the pot with any accumulated juices and add the thyme and 1 cup water.
7. Bring the liquid to a boil and then reduce the heat to low so that the liquid simmers.
8. Cover and simmer for about 4½ hours or until the beef is very tender.
9. In a small bowl, stir together the cornstarch and 3 tbsp water to form a slurry.
10. Whisk the slurry into the liquid in the pot and cook for 15 minutes to thicken the sauce.
11. Serve the roast with the gravy.

Per Serving

Calories: **159** | Fat: **10g** | Carbs: **2g** | Fiber: **3g** | Phosphorus: **109mg** | Potassium: **184mg** | Sodium: **44mg** | Protein: **14g**

SPICY PORK TENDERLOIN

Prep time: **2 hours and 15 minutes** | Cook time:
1 hour and 10 minutes | Serves **4**

- 2 lbs pork loin roast (boneless)
- 3-4 cloves garlic - minced
- ½ tsp ground black pepper
- 2 tsp allspice
- 2 tsp onion powder
- ½ tsp cumin
- 2 t vegetable oil

1. Mix the minced garlic, allspice, black pepper, cumin and onion powder, and then brush the tenderloin.
2. Add in a bowl for two hours. Cover and chill.
3. Heat the oven to 300°F.
4. Drizzle the oil from the vegetables in the roasting pan.
5. Place the tenderloin and shake over the pork with all the leftover ingredients.
6. Roast for 45 min. To 1 h. Uncovered.

Per Serving

Calories: **412** | Protein: **56g** | Carbs: **12g** | Fat: **21g** | Fiber: **0g** | Sodium: **214mg** | Potassium: **345mg** | Phosphorus: **212mg**

TORTILLA BEEF ROLLUPS

Prep time: **10 minutes** | Cook time: **0 minutes** | Serves **4**

- 8 slices of cucumber
- 2 flour tortilla (6" size)
- ¼ bell pepper you can take red, green, or yellow cut in strips
- 2 tbsp cream cheese (whipped)
- 1 tbsp herb seasoning blend
- 2 romaine lettuce leaves
- 5 ounces cooked roast beef
- ¼ cup chopped red onion

1. Place a layer of cream cheese on top of the tortillas.
2. Divide the ingredients in two to create two tortillas. Place the roast beef, red onion, bell pepper strips, cucumbers and lettuce in each tortilla.
3. Sprinkle with the herb seasoning.
4. Roll up like a jelly roll.
5. Cut each tortilla into 4 pieces, or serve whole.

Per Serving

Calories: **514** | Protein: **53g** | Carbs: **48g** | Fat: **31.8g** | Fiber: **6g** | Sodium: **61mg** | Potassium: **378mg** | Phosphorus: **108mg**

BARBECUE BEEF

Prep time: **15 minutes** | Cook time: **4 hours and 30 minutes** | Serves **4**

- 2 lbs of beef roast for
- Barbeque
- 1 tsp black pepper
- 1 onion, chopped into large slices
- 1 clove garlic
- 1 laurel (bay leaf)
- 1 chile de arbol
- ¼ Chipotle chile

1. Inside the strips, cut the meat and rinse it.
2. Rinse and pat until completely dry.
3. Place in crockpot/oven roasting bag.
4. Add onion, pepper, bay leaf, garlic and chiles to a blender. Blend thoroughly.
5. Place in the slow cooker with the beef strips.
6. Remove the air (if used) from the cooking bag and seal as tightly as necessary.
7. Cook on high until boiling for one hour, then lower the heat and cook for four hours.

Per Serving

Calories: **432** | Protein: **23g** | Carbs: **38g** | Fat: **21.8g** | Fiber: **2g** | Sodium: **55mg** | Potassium: **678mg** | Phosphorus: **308mg**

SPICED UP PORK CHOPS

Prep time: **4 hours 10 minutes** | Cook time: **15 minutes** | Serves **4**

- ¼ cup lime juice
- 4 pork rib chops
- 1 tbsp coconut oil, melted
- 2 garlic cloves, peeled and minced
- 1 tbsp chili powder
- 1 tsp ground
- cinnamon
- 2 tsp cumin
- Salt and pepper to taste
- ½ tsp hot pepper sauce
- Mango, sliced

1. Take a bowl and mix in lime juice, oil, garlic, cumin, cinnamon, chili powder, salt, pepper, hot pepper sauce
2. Whisk well
3. Add pork chops and toss
4. Keep it on the side and refrigerate for 4 hours
5. Pre-heat your grill to medium and transfer pork chops to a pre-heated grill
6. Grill for 7 minutes both sides
7. Divide between serving platters and serve with mango slices
8. Enjoy!

Per Serving

Calories: **318** | Protein: **31g** | Carbs: **5g** | Fat: **20g** | Fiber: **2g** | Sodium: **110mg** | Potassium: **500mg** | Phosphorus: **220mg**

STEAK AND ONION SANDWICH

Prep time: **25 minutes** | Cook time: **8 minutes** | Serves **4**

- 4 flank steaks (around 4 oz. each)
- 1 medium red onion, sliced
- 1 tbsp. of lemon juice
- 1 tbsp. of Italian
- seasoning
- 1 tsp. of black pepper
- 1 tbsp. of vegetable oil
- 4 sandwich/burger buns

1. Wrap the steak with the lemon juice, the Italian seasoning, and pepper to taste. Cut into 4 pieces Heat the vegetable oil in a medium skillet over medium heat.
2. Cook steaks around 3 minutes on each side until you get a medium to well-done result. Take off and transfer onto a dish with absorbing paper.
3. In the same skillet, saute the onions until tender and transparent (around 3 minutes).
4. Cut the sandwich bun into half and place 1 piece of steak in each topped with the onions. Serve or wrap with paper or foil and keep in the fridge for the next day.

Per Serving

Calories: **315.26** | Carbs: **8.47g** | Protein: **38.33g** | Sodium: **266.24mg** | Potassium: **238.2mg** | Phosphorus: **364.25mg** | Fiber: **0.76g** | Fat: **13.22g**

ITALIAN STYLE LAMB PATTIES

Perp time: **5 minutes** | Cook time: **10 minutes** | Serves **4**

- 1 lb of ground lean lamb
- ½ cup of feta cheese, crumbled
- 1 clove of garlic, minced
- ½ tsp of dried oregano
- ½ tsp of crushed black pepper
- ¼ cup of white onion, chopped
- ¼ cup of panko breadcrumbs

1. Combine the lamb with all the ingredients in a large bowl.
2. Shape into 4 patties of equal size (around ½ inch thick).
3. Heat a grilling and non-stick pan over medium heat with cooking spray.
4. Add the lamb patties and let them cook on high heat for nearly 5 minutes on each side. Ensure that the patties are no pink in the center by cutting one in half.
5. Serve

Per Serving

Calories: **118.39** | Carbs: **2.1 g** | Protein: **7.5 g** | Sodium: **88.4 mg** | Potassium: **9.93 mg** | Phosphorus: **21.82 mg** | Fiber: **0.8 g** | Fat: **9.2 g**

MEATLOAF WITH MUSHROOM GRAVY

Prep time: **10 minutes** | Cook time: **50 minutes** | Serves **8**

- nonstick cooking spray
- 1 tbsp plus 1 tsp extra-virgin olive oil, divided
- 1 (8-ounce) package sliced cremini mushrooms
- 1 tsp dried oregano
- 1 sweet onion, finely chopped
- 3 garlic cloves, minced
- 1½ pounds lean ground beef
- 1 large egg
- 1 slice white bread, pulsed in a food processor into coarse bread crumbs
- ¼ tsp freshly ground black pepper
- 1 tbsp all-purpose flour
- 1 cup low-sodium beef broth

1. Preheat the oven to 350°F. Coat a loaf pan with nonstick cooking spray.
2. In a large skillet over medium-high heat, heat 1 tbsp of olive oil. Add the mushrooms and oregano. Cook for 5 minutes, stirring occasionally. Add the onion and garlic, and continue to cook for 5 minutes, until the mushrooms and onion are soft. Remove from the heat. Divide the mushroom mixture into two equal parts, and finely chop one part. Set the other part aside.
3. In a medium bowl, add the chopped-mushroom mixture, beef, egg, bread crumbs, and pepper. Mix well. Form the beef mixture into a loaf and transfer it into the loaf pan. Bake for 45 minutes, until cooked through.
4. In a saucepan over medium-high heat, heat the remaining 1 tsp of olive oil, and add the remaining mushroom mixture. Stir in the flour and mix to coat. Slowly add the broth, stirring constantly to break up any clumps. Bring to a boil, reduce the heat, and simmer for 5 minutes, until thickened. Spoon the gravy over slices of meatloaf, and serve.

Per Serving

Calories: **280** | Fat: **20g** | Carbs: **7g** | Fiber: **1g** | Protein: **17g** | Phosphorus: **192mg** | Potassium: **394mg** | Sodium: **146mg**

GRILLED SKIRT STEAK

Prep time: **15 minutes** | Cook time: **8-9 minutes** | Serves **4**

- 2 tsp fresh ginger herb, grated finely
- 2 tsp fresh lime zest, grated finely
- ¼ cup coconut sugar
- 2 tsp fish sauce
- 2 tbsp fresh lime juice
- ½ cup coconut almond milk
- 1-pound beef skirt steak, trimmed and cut into 4-inch slices lengthwise
- Salt, to taste

1. In a sizable sealable bag, mix together all ingredients except steak and salt.
2. Add steak and coat with marinade generously.
3. Seal the bag and refrigerate to marinate for about 4-12 hours.
4. Preheat the grill to high heat. Grease the grill grate.
5. Remove steak from refrigerator and discard the marinade.
6. with a paper towel, dry the steak and sprinkle with salt evenly.
7. Cook the steak for approximately 3½ minutes.
8. Flip the medial side and cook for around 2½-5 minutes or till desired doneness.
9. Remove from grill pan and keep side for approximately 5 minutes before slicing.
10. with a clear, crisp knife cut into desired slices and serve.

Per Serving

Calories: **465** | Fat: **10g** | Carbs: **22g** | Fiber: **0g** | Protein: **37g** | Sodium: **300mg** | Potassium: **400mg** | Phosphorus: **200mg**

ITALIAN STYLE MEATBALLS

Prep time: **15 minutes** | Cook time: **35 minutes** | Serves **4**

- olive oil cooking spray
- 12 ounces lean ground beef
- 1 egg
- 2 tbsp bread crumbs
- 2 tbsp grated Parmesan cheese
- 1 tbsp chopped fresh parsley
- 1 tsp minced garlic
- ½ tsp Dijon mustard
- pinch freshly ground black pepper

1. Preheat the oven to 350°F.
2. Lightly coat a baking sheet with cooking spray.
3. In a large bowl, mix together the beef, egg, bread crumbs, Parmesan cheese, parsley, garlic, mustard, and pepper.
4. Form the meat mixture into small (1-inch) meatballs, and arrange them on the prepared baking sheet.
5. Bake until browned, turning several times, about 35 minutes.
6. Serve hot.

Per Serving

Calories: **159** | Fat: **6g** | Sodium: **143mg** | Carbs: **3g** | Fiber: **0g** | Phosphorus: **206mg** | Potassium: **311mg** | Protein: **21g**

STUFFING OF TACOS WITH BEEF

Prep time: **5 minutes** | Cook time: **25 minutes** | Serves **4**

- 2 tbsp vegetable oil
- 1 ¼ pounds lean ground beef
- ½ tsp ground red pepper
- ½ tsp black pepper
- 1 tsp Italian seasoning
- 1 tsp garlic powder
- 1 tsp onion powder
- ½ tsp Tabasco sauce
- ½ tsp nutmeg

Will Also Need:

- 1 medium taco shells
- ½ head shredded lettuce

1. Heat the oil. Put the minced meat and all the leftover ingredients, except the lettuce and the tacos.
2. In a skillet, cook until the meat as well as the ingredients are well mixed.
3. Fill taco shells with 4 tbsp of meat and top with shredded lettuce.

Per Serving

Calories: **167** | Protein: **3g** | Carbs: **31g** | Fat: **6g** | Fiber: **5g** | Sodium: **86mg** | Potassium: **321mg** | Phosphorus: **188mg**

CHAPTER 8: SEAFOOD MAINS

GARLIC-BUTTER CRAB PASTA

Prep time: **5 minutes** | Cook time: **20 minutes** | Serves **4**

- 4 ounces orzo
- 1 tbsp olive oil
- 1 small white onion, diced
- 4 garlic cloves, minced
- 1 medium red bell pepper, diced
- 2 tbsp dried oregano
- 1 tsp freshly ground black pepper
- 1 tbsp unsalted butter
- 1 tbsp lemon juice
- 4 (4¼-ounce) cans crabmeat

1. Cook the orzo as directed on the package. Set aside.
2. In a medium skillet, heat the oil over medium heat. Add the onion, garlic, and bell pepper and cook until the vegetables are tender and the onion is translucent, about 3 minutes.
3. Add the oregano, black pepper, butter, lemon juice, and crabmeat and stir to combine.
4. Add the cooked orzo and stir until all the ingredients are incorporated, then cook until warmed through, about 3 minutes.
5. Remove the skillet from the heat and serve.

Per Serving

Calories: **303** | Protein: **19g** | Fat: **7g** | Carbs: **34g** | Fiber: **3g** | Phosphorus: **302mg** | Potassium: **413mg** | Sodium: **482mg**

SEARED HERBED SCALLOPS

Prep time: **15 minutes** | Cook time: **5 minutes** | Serves **4**

- 1 tbsp olive oil
- 12 ounces sea scallops, rinsed and patted dry
- freshly ground black pepper
- 2 tbsp freshly squeezed lemon juice
- 1 tsp chopped fresh parsley
- 1 tsp chopped fresh thyme
- 1 tsp chopped fresh chives

1. In a large skillet over medium-high heat, heat the olive oil.
2. Lightly season the scallops with pepper. Add them to the skillet.
3. Sear the scallops, turning once, until just cooked through and browned, about 4 minutes total.
4. Stir in the lemon juice, parsley, thyme, and chives.
5. Turn the scallops to coat in the herb sauce.
6. Serve hot.

Per Serving

Calories: **131** | Fat: **5g** | Sodium: **136mg** | Carbs: **2g** | Fiber: **0g** | Phosphorus: **176mg** | Potassium: **268mg** | Protein: **14g**

TUNA SALAD

Prep time: **10 minutes** | Cook time: **0 minutes** | Serves **4**

- 12 oz low sodium canned tuna
- ¼ c. red onion, chopped
- ¼ c. red pepper, chopped
- ¼ c. celery, chopped
- 2 t. ken's honey mustard dipping sauce

1. Mince the red pepper, celery and red onion into small bits.
2. Mix it with honey mustard and tuna.

Per Serving

Calories: **289** | Protein: **31g** | Carbs: **27g** | Fat: **16g** | Fiber: **9g** | Sodium: **143mg** | Potassium: **364mg** | Phosphorus: **321mg**

MACKEREL MUSHROOM RISOTTO

Prep time: **8 minutes** | Cook time: **22 minutes** | Serves **6**

- 4 cups low-sodium vegetable broth
- 1 (4.4-ounce) can atlantic mackerel in oil
- 1 onion, chopped
- 1 (8-ounce) package sliced cremini mushrooms
- 2 garlic cloves, minced
- 1½ cups arborio rice or long-grain white rice
- juice of 1 lemon
- 2 tbsp unsalted butter
- 2 tbsp grated parmesan cheese

1. Bring the broth to a simmer in a small saucepan over low heat. Set aside and cover to keep warm.
2. Drain the mackerel, reserving the oil. Put 2 tbsp of the oil into a large saucepan and heat over medium heat.
3. Add the onion and mushrooms and sauté for 2 minutes.
4. Stir in the garlic and rice and sauté for 2 minutes.
5. Start adding the broth to the rice mixture, about ½ cup at a time, stirring constantly.
6. When the broth is absorbed, add more broth. You can stir less often as the rice begins to cook but keep an eye on the pan.
7. The risotto is done when the rice is tender and most of the broth is absorbed, about 20 minutes in total. You may not need all of the broth. This dish can be soupier or thicker, depending on how much broth you add and your taste.
8. Stir in the reserved mackerel, lemon juice, butter, and cheese and serve immediately.

Per Serving

Calories: **270** | Fat: **6g** | Sodium: **213mg** | Potassium: **334mg** | Phosphorus: **187mg** | Carbs: **43g** | Fiber: **1g** | Protein: **10g**

SALMON AND PESTO SALAD

Prep time: **5 minutes** | Cook time: **15 minutes** | Serves **2**

For The Pesto:
- 1 minced garlic clove
- ½ cup fresh arugula
- ¼ cup extra virgin olive oil
- ½ cup fresh basil
- 1 tsp black pepper

For The Salmon:
- 4 oz. skinless salmon fillet
- 1 tbsp coconut oil

For The Salad:
- ½ juiced lemon
- 2 sliced radishes
- ½ cup iceberg lettuce
- 1 tsp black pepper

1. Prepare the pesto by blending all the pesto ingredients in a food processor or by grinding with a pestle and mortar. Set aside.
2. Add a skillet to the stove on medium-high heat and melt the coconut oil.
3. Add the salmon to the pan.
4. Cook for 7-8 minutes and turn over.
5. Cook for a further 3-4 minutes or until cooked through.
6. Remove fillets from the skillet and allow to rest.
7. Mix the lettuce and the radishes and squeeze over the juice of ½ lemon.
8. Flake the salmon with a fork and mix through the salad.
9. Toss to coat and sprinkle with a little black pepper to serve.

Per Serving

Calories: **221g** | Protein: **13 g** | Carbs: **1 g** | Fiber: **4g** | Fat: **34 g** | Sodium: **80 mg** | Potassium: **119 mg** | Phosphorus: **158 mg**

LEMON POACHED SALMON

Prep time: **5 minutes** | Cook time: **15 minutes** | Serves **4**

- 1 cup water
- juice and zest of 1 lemon
- 2 tbsp chopped fresh thyme
- 1 tbsp chopped fresh dill
- 6 peppercorns
- 4 (3-ounce) skinless salmon fillets

1. In a large skillet over medium-high heat, add the water, lemon juice, lemon zest, thyme, dill, and peppercorns.
2. Bring the liquid to a boil, then reduce the heat to low and simmer. Add the salmon fillets to the skillet and cover.
3. Poach the salmon until opaque and cooked through, about 15 minutes.
4. Transfer the salmon to a plate, and discard the poaching liquid.
5. Serve the fish hot or cold.

Per Serving

Calories: **150** | Fat: **9g** | Sodium: **39mg** | Carbs: **0g** | Fiber: **0g** | Phosphorus: **243mg** | Potassium: **331mg** | Protein: **17g**

TANGY GLAZED BLACK COD

Prep time:**10 minutes** | Cook time: **15 minutes** | Serves **4**

- 3 tbsp fresh lime juice
- 2 tbsp honey
- 2 tbsp vinegar
- 1 tbsp soy sauce
- 1 (1 pound) fillet black cod, bones removed

1. Preheat oven to 425 °F. Spray the bottom of a Dutch oven or covered casserole dish with cooking spray.
2. Combine lime juice, honey, vinegar, and soy sauce in a saucepan over medium heat; cook and stir until sauce is thickened, about 5 minutes.
3. Place cod in the prepared Dutch oven. Pour sauce over fish Cover dish with an oven-safe lid.
4. Bake in the preheated oven until fish flakes easily with a fork, about 10 minutes.

Per Serving

Calories: **44** | Fat: **0g** | Sodium: **127mg** | Carbs: **11.8g** | Fiber: **0.2g** | Protein: **0.5g** | Potassium: **58mg** | Potassium: **40mg**

SALMON AND CARROTS MIX

Prep time: **10 minutes** | Cook time:**10minutes** | Serves **4**

- 4 oz. chopped smoked salmon
- 1 tbsp. essential olive oil
- Black pepper
- 1 tbsp. chopped chives
- ¼ c. coconut cream
- 1 ½ lbs. chopped carrots
- 2 tsps. Prepared horseradish

1. Heat up a pan using the oil over medium heat, add carrots and cook for 10 minutes.
2. Add salmon, chives, horseradish, cream and black pepper, toss, cook for 1 minute more, divide between plates and serve.
3. Enjoy!

Per Serving

Calories:**233** | Protein: **7g** | Carbs: **16g** | Fat: **15g** | Fiber: **5g** | Sodium: **600mg** | Potassium: **700mg** | Phosphorus: **100mg**

HERB PESTO TUNA

Prep time: **10 minutes** | Cook time: **10 minutes** | Serves **4**

- 4 (3-ounce) yellowfin tuna fillets
- 1 tsp olive oil
- freshly ground black pepper
- ¼ cup herb pesto (see)
- 1 lemon, cut into 8 thin slices

1. Heat the barbecue to medium-high.
2. Drizzle the fish with the olive oil and season each fillet with pepper.
3. Cook the fish on the barbecue for 4 minutes.
4. Turn the fish over and top each piece with the herb pesto and lemon slices.
5. Grill for 5 to 6 minutes more or until the tuna is cooked to medium-well.

Per Serving

Calories: **103** | Fat: **2g** | Carbs: **0g** | Fiber: **4g** | Phosphorus: **236mg** | Potassium: **374mg** | Sodium: **38mg** | Protein: **21g**

SCALLOPS AND STRAWBERRY MIX

Prep time: **20 minutes** | Cook time: **30minutes** | Serves **2**

- 1 tbsp. lime juice
- ½ c. Pico de Gallo
- Black pepper
- 4 oz. scallops
- ½ c. chopped strawberries

1. Heat up a pan over medium heat, add scallops, cook for 3 minutes on both sides and take away heat,
2. In a bowl, mix strawberries with lime juice, Pico de gallo, scallops and pepper, toss and serve cold.
3. Enjoy!

Per Serving

Calories: **169** | Fat: **2 g** | Carbs: **8 g** | Protein: **13 g** | Fiber: **3g** | Sodium: **235.7 mg** | Potassium: **250mg** | Phosphorus: **130mg**

WHITE FISH AND BROCCOLI CURRY

Prep time: 10 minutes | Cook time: 10 minutes | Serves 6

For The Curry Paste:

- ½ sweet onion, chopped
- 1 medium red chile, chopped
- 1-inch piece ginger, peeled and chopped
- 1 lemongrass stalk, outer leaves removed, tender bottom portion chopped
- ¼ cup roughly chopped fresh cilantro stems
- 1 tsp turmeric powder
- ½ tsp cumin seeds
- 2 tbsp extra-virgin olive oil

For The Curry:

- ¾ cup homemade rice milk or unsweetened store-bought rice milk
- ½ cup cream cheese
- 1 pound tilapia fillets
- 3 cups broccoli florets
- juice of 1 lime
- 1 tsp sugar

To Make The Curry Paste:

1. Using a mortar and pestle or blender, combine the onion, chile, ginger, lemongrass, cilantro, turmeric, cumin seeds, and olive oil, and blend until smooth.

To Make The Curry:

1. In a large skillet over medium-high heat, heat the curry paste, and cook, stirring occasionally, for 2 to 3 minutes, until fragrant. Add the rice milk and stir until incorporated. Bring to a light simmer.
2. Meanwhile, in a small bowl, add the cream cheese. Add a few tbsp of the hot rice-milk mixture and stir until blended.
3. Add the tilapia and broccoli to the skillet, then add the cream-cheese mixture, gently stirring to blend.
4. Cook for 3 to 5 minutes, until the fish is cooked through, the broccoli is fork-tender, and the curry is bubbly. Stir in the lime juice and sugar. Remove from the heat, and serve over white rice.

Per Serving

Calories: **223** | Fat: **13g** | | Carbs: **10g** | Fiber: **2g** | Protein: **18g** | Phosphorus: **194mg** | Potassium: **490mg** | Sodium: **134mg**

CHAPTER 9:
VEGETARIAN DISHES

SPINACH FALAFEL WRAP

Prep time: **10 minutes** | Cook time: **15 minutes** | Serves **4**

- 6 ounces baby spinach
- 1 (15-ounce) can chickpeas, drained and rinsed
- 2 tsp ground cumin
- ¾ cup flour
- 2 tbsp canola oil, divided, for frying
- ¼ cup plain, unsweetened yogurt
- 2 garlic cloves, minced
- juice of 1 lemon
- freshly ground black pepper
- 4 tortillas
- 1 cucumber, cut into spears
- 2 slices red onion
- salad greens, for serving

1. Place the spinach in a colander in the sink, and pour boiling water over it to wilt the spinach. Allow it to cool, then press as much water out of the spinach as possible.
2. In a food processor, add the spinach, chickpeas, cumin, and flour. Pulse until just blended.
3. Divide the mixture into tbsp-size balls, and use your hands to press them flat into patties.
4. In a large skillet over medium-high heat, heat 1 tbsp of oil. Add half of the falafel patties, and cook for 2 to 3 minutes on each side, until browned and crisp. Repeat with the remaining falafel patties.
5. In a small bowl, combine the yogurt, garlic, lemon juice, and pepper.
6. On each tortilla, place 3 falafel patties, a couple cucumber spears, a few red-onion rings, and a handful of salad greens. Top each with 1 tbsp of the yogurt sauce.

Per Serving

Calories: **241** | Fat: **7g** | Carbs: **37g** | Fiber: **4g** | Protein: **8g** | Phosphorus: **110mg** | Potassium: **245mg** | Sodium: **285mg**

TOFU AND EGGPLANT STIR-FRY

Prep time: **20 minutes** | Cook time: **20 minutes** | Serves **4**

- 1 tbsp granulated sugar
- 1 tbsp all-purpose flour
- 1 tsp grated fresh ginger
- 1 tsp minced garlic
- 1 tsp minced jalapeño pepper
- juice of 1 lime
- water
- 2 tbsp olive oil, divided
- 5 ounces extra-firm tofu, cut into ½-inch cubes
- 2 cups cubed eggplant
- 2 scallions, both green and white parts, sliced
- 3 tbsp chopped cilantro

1. In a small bowl, whisk together the sugar, flour, ginger, garlic, jalapeño, lime juice, and enough water to make ⅔ cup of sauce; set aside.
2. In a large skillet over medium-high heat, heat 1 tbsp of the oil.
3. Sauté the tofu for about 6 minutes or until it is crisp and golden.
4. Remove the tofu; set aside on a plate.
5. Add the remaining 1 tbsp oil and sauté the eggplant cubes for about 10 minutes or until they are fully cooked and lightly browned.
6. Add the tofu and scallions to the skillet and toss to combine.
7. Pour in the sauce and bring to a boil, stirring constantly, for about 2 minutes or until the sauce is thickened.
8. Add the cilantro before serving.

Per Serving

Calories: **386** | Fat: **22g** | Carbs: **37g** | Fiber: **3g** | Phosphorus: **120mg** | Potassium: **146mg** | Sodium: **219mg** | Protein: **10g**

VEGGIE CABBAGE STIR-FRY

Prep time: **20 minutes** | Cook time: **10 minutes** | Serves **4**

- 1 cup low-sodium vegetable broth
- 1 tbsp cornstarch
- 2 tsp low-sodium soy sauce
- ½ tsp ground ginger
- 2 tbsp olive oil
- 4 cups chopped cabbage
- 1 (8-ounce) package sliced mushrooms
- 2 cups grated carrots
- 2 garlic cloves, sliced
- 3 cups cooked brown rice

1. In a small bowl, stir together the broth, cornstarch, soy sauce, and ginger; set aside.
2. Heat the olive oil in a wok or large skillet over medium heat.
3. Stir-fry the cabbage for 3 minutes.
4. Stir in the mushrooms, carrots, and garlic and stir-fry for another 2 minutes.
5. Add the broth mixture to the skillet. Stir until the sauce bubbles and thickens and the cabbage is tender, 4 to 5 minutes.
6. Serve the stir-fry over the rice.

Per Serving

Calories: **307** | Fat **9g** | Sodium: **174mg** | Potassium: **579mg** | Phosphorus: **247mg** | Carbs: **52g** | Fiber: **6g** | Protein: **8g**

BROCCOLI-ONION LATKES

Prep time: **15 minutes** | Cook time: **20 minutes** | Serves **4**

- 3 cups broccoli florets, diced
- ½ cup onion, chopped
- 2 large eggs, beaten
- 2 tbsp. all-purpose white flour
- 2 tbsp. olive oil

1. Cook the broccoli for around 5 minutes until tender. Drain.
2. Mix the flour into the eggs.
3. Combine the onion, broccoli, and egg mixture and stir through.
4. Prepare olive oil in a skillet on medium-high heat.
5. Drop a spoon of the mixture onto the pan to make 4 latkes.
6. Cook each side until golden brown.
7. Drain on a paper towel and serve.

Per Serving

Calories: **140** | Carbs: **7g** | Carbs: **8g** | Protein: **6g** | Fiber: **2g** | Sodium: **58mg** | Potassium: **276mg** | Phosphorous: **101mg**

BULGUR VEGETABLE SALAD

Prep time: **15 minutes** | Cook time: **10 minutes** | Serves **5**

- 1 cup cooked bulgur
- 1 cup chopped broccoli
- 1 cup chopped cauliflower
- 1 red bell pepper, finely diced
- 1 scallion, white and green parts, chopped
- 2 tbsp chopped fresh basil leaves
- juice and zest of 1 lemon
- 1 tbsp olive oil
- freshly ground black pepper

1. In a large bowl, toss together the bulgur, broccoli, cauliflower, bell pepper, scallion, basil, lemon juice, lemon zest, and olive oil. Season with pepper.
2. Toss again and serve.

Per Serving

Calories: **117** | Fat: **3g** | Sodium: **15mg** | Carbs: **21g** | Fiber: **4g** | Phosphorus: **59mg** | Potassium: **199mg** | Protein: **2g**

BLACK BEAN BURGERS

Prep time: **10 minutes** | Cook time: **10 minutes** | Serves **4**

- 1 (15-ounce) can no-added-salt black beans, drained and rinsed
- 2 tbsp olive oil, divided
- 1 tbsp lemon juice
- 1 tbsp dried oregano
- 2 garlic cloves, minced
- ½ cup rolled (old-fashioned) oats
- Tzatziki Sauce
- 4 hamburger buns
- 8 cucumber slices
- 4 tomato slices

1. Combine the black beans, 1 tbsp of the oil, the lemon juice, oregano, and garlic in a food processor and pulse 3 or 4 times, until the beans are smashed. (Alternatively, combine the ingredients in a bowl and use a potato masher to smash the beans.)
2. Add the oats and stir until well combined. Using your hands, form the mixture into four equal-size patties.
3. In a medium skillet, heat the remaining 1 tbsp oil over medium heat. Add the patties and cook for 3 minutes per side, or until golden brown.
4. Divide the tzatziki sauce evenly among the buns, spreading it over the cut sides of the top and bottom halves of each. Top each bottom bun with a black bean patty, two cucumber slices, and a tomato slice, then finish with the bun tops.

Per Serving

Calories: **314** | Protein: **12g** | Fat: **10g** | Carbs: **46g** | Fiber: **8g** | Phosphorus: **203mg** | Potassium: **371mg** | Sodium: **212mg**

LIME ASPARAGUS SPAGHETTI

Prep time: **5 minutes** | Cook time: **20 minutes** | Serves **6**

- 1 pound asparagus spears, trimmed and cut into 2-inch pieces
- 2 tsp olive oil
- 2 tsp minced garlic
- 2 tsp all-purpose flour
- 1 cup Homemade Rice Milk (, or use unsweetened store-bought) or almond milk
- juice and zest of ½ lemon
- 1 tbsp chopped fresh thyme
- freshly ground black pepper
- 2 cups cooked spaghetti
- ¼ cup grated Parmesan cheese

1. Fill a large saucepan with water and bring to a boil over high heat. Add the asparagus and blanch until crisp-tender, about 2 minutes. Drain and set aside.
2. In a large skillet over medium-high heat, heat the olive oil. Add the garlic, and sauté until softened, about 2 minutes. Whisk in the flour to create a paste, about 1 minute. Whisk in the rice milk, lemon juice, lemon zest, and thyme.
3. Reduce the heat to medium and cook the sauce, whisking constantly, until thickened and creamy, about 3 minutes.
4. Season the sauce with pepper.
5. Stir in the spaghetti and the asparagus.
6. Serve the pasta topped with the Parmesan cheese.

Per Serving

Calories: **127** | Fat: **3g** | Sodium: **67mg** | Carbs: **19g** | Fiber: **2g** | Phosphorus: **109mg** | Potassium: **200mg** | Protein: **6g**

VEGETARIAN SHEPHERD'S PIE

Prep time: 5 minutes | Cook time: 35 minutes | Serves 2

- 2 cups mixed frozen vegetables boiled in water
- 1 can tin lentils water drained
- Ground black pepper
- 16-ounce canned chickpeas drained water
- 1 cup canned chopped tomatoes drained water
- 1 tsp paprika
- 1 pinch of dried mixed herbs
- 1 cup couscous
- ¼ cup grated hard cheese

1. Put the mixed fresh veggies in a pan with cold water and bring them to a boil.
2. Cook, rinse and dispose of the water for 5 minutes. Meanwhile, except for the couscous and cheese, place other ingredients into a pan and heat through.
3. Add the vegetables that have been cooked. Put it in a bowl that is oven-resistant.
4. Cook the couscous and scatter over the bowl according to the instructions on the box.
5. with the cheese and barbecue, sprinkle over the couscous until golden brown. Serve (crusty) with bread.

Per Serving

Calories: **321** | Protein: **21g** | Carbs: **35g** | Fat: **9g** | Fiber: **3g** | Sodium: **85mg** | Potassium: **364mg** | Phosphorus: **139mg**

GERMAN BRAISED CABBAGE

Prep time: 15 minutes | Cook time: 15 minutes | Serves 4

- 1 tbsp olive oil
- 5 cups shredded red cabbage
- 1 pear, peeled, cored, and chopped
- ¼ large sweet onion, chopped
- 3 tbsp apple cider vinegar
- 1 tbsp sugar
- ½ tsp caraway seed
- ½ tsp dry mustard

1. In a large skillet over medium-high heat, heat the olive oil.
2. Add the cabbage, pear, and onion, and sauté until tender, about 10 minutes.
3. In a small bowl, stir together the vinegar, sugar, caraway seed, and mustard.
4. Pour the vinegar mixture into the cabbage and stir to combine. Cover and simmer the cabbage for 5 minutes.
5. Serve hot.

Per Serving

Calories: **62** | Fat: **2g** | Sodium: **14mg** | Carbs: **10g** | Fiber: **3g** | Phosphorus: **23mg** | Potassium: **161mg** | Protein: **1g**

MIXED GREEN LEAF AND CITRUS SALAD

Prep time: 10 minutes | Cook time: 15 minutes | Serves 4

- 4 cups mixed salad greens
- ¼ cup pepitas
- juice of 1 lemon
- 2 tsp extra-virgin olive oil
- freshly ground black pepper
- 1 orange, peeled and thinly sliced
- ½ lemon, peeled and thinly sliced
- 4 tbsp (¼ cup) dried cranberries
- 4 tbsp (¼ cup) pitted kalamata olives

1. In a large bowl, toss the greens, pepitas, lemon juice, and olive oil. Season with pepper.
2. Arrange the greens on four plates, and top each with 2 slices of orange and lemon. Add 1 tbsp each of cranberries and Kalamata olives to each plate. Serve.

Per Serving

Calories: **142** | Fat: **9g** | Carbs: **15g** | Fiber: **2g** | Protein: **3g** | Phosphorus: **116mg** | Potassium: **219mg** | Sodium: **137mg**

BARLEY AND ROASTED VEGETABLE BOWL

Prep time: **10 minutes** | Cook time: **30 minutes** | Serves **4**

- 2 small asian eggplants, diced
- 2 small zucchini, diced
- ½ red bell pepper, chopped
- ½ sweet onion, cut into wedges
- 2 tbsp extra-virgin olive oil, divided
- freshly ground black pepper
- 1 cup barley
- juice of 1 lemon
- 3 garlic cloves, minced
- ¼ cup basil leaves, roughly chopped
- ¼ cup crumbled feta cheese
- 2 cups arugula or mixed baby salad greens

1. Preheat the oven to 425°F.
2. In a medium bowl, toss the eggplant, zucchini, bell pepper, and onion with 1 tbsp of olive oil, and arrange the vegetables in a single layer on a baking sheet. Season with pepper.
3. Roast the vegetables for about 25 minutes, stirring once or twice, until they are browned and tender. Set aside.
4. Meanwhile, in a medium pot, add the barley and 2 cups of water. Bring to a boil, reduce the heat to simmer, cover, and cook for 20 minutes. Turn off the heat, and let rest for 10 minutes. Fluff with a fork, and drain any remaining water.
5. In a small bowl, whisk the lemon juice, garlic, and remaining tbsp of olive oil.
6. Toss the vegetables with the barley, and then mix together with the lemon-garlic dressing. Right before serving, stir in the basil, feta cheese, and salad greens.

Per Serving

Calories: **292** | Fat: **10g** | Carbs: **44g** | Fiber: **11g** | Protein: **9g** | Phosphorus: **201mg** | Potassium: **543mg** | Sodium: **119mg**

VEGETARIAN ENCHILADAS

Prep time: **10 minutes** | Cook time: **35 minutes** | Serves **8**

- avocado or olive oil cooking spray
- 2 tbsp avocado or olive oil
- 2 cups diced zucchini
- 1 (10-ounce) package frozen corn
- 1 small red onion, diced
- 1 (15-ounce) can no-salt-added or low-sodium black beans, drained and rinsed
- 3 cups enchilada sauce or store-bought, divided
- 8 (10-inch) whole-wheat tortillas
- 2 cups shredded low-sodium mozzarella or mexican-blend cheese
- handful chopped cilantro, for garnish (optional)

1. Preheat the oven to 350°F. Coat a 13-by-9-inch baking dish with cooking spray and set aside.
2. In a large skillet or pan, heat the oil over medium-high heat. Add the zucchini, corn, and onion and sauté until the vegetables are soft, about 5 minutes. Add the beans, stir gently, and cook for an additional 1 to 2 minutes. Remove from the heat.
3. Spread about 1 cup of the enchilada sauce on the bottom of the baking dish. Take 1 tortilla and spread about ½ cup of the bean mixture onto the center of the tortilla. Sprinkle about 2 tbsp of cheese and roll up the tortilla. Place the tortilla seam-side down in the baking dish. Repeat with all of the tortillas.
4. Sprinkle with the remaining ¼ cup cheese and top with the remaining enchilada sauce. Cover with foil and bake for 20 minutes. Uncover and bake for an additional 10 minutes. Garnish with cilantro (if using) and serve.
5. Store leftovers in an airtight container in the refrigerator for up to 5 days or in the freezer for up to 3 months.

Per Serving

Calories: **316** | Protein: **15.3g** | Carbs: **39g** | Fiber: **9g** | Fat: **13g** | Saturated Fat: **5g** | Sodium: **318mg** | Potassium: **453mg** | Phosphorus: **204mg**

CHAPTER 10: SOUPS AND STEWS

ROASTED VEGGIE GINGER SOUP

Prep time: **10 minutes** | Cook time: **50 minutes** | Serves **10**

- 3 cups spaghetti squash, peeled and cubed
- 6 medium carrots, peeled and quartered
- 1 garlic head, top cut off to expose the cloves inside
- avocado or olive oil cooking spray
- 2 tbsp olive or avocado oil
- 1 medium yellow onion, diced
- 2 tbsp grated fresh ginger
- 1 tsp ground cumin
- ½ tsp dried oregano
- ½ tsp dried thyme
- dash freshly ground black pepper
- dash salt
- 6 cups no-salt-added or low-sodium vegetable broth

1. Preheat the oven to 425°F. Line a baking sheet with parchment paper and arrange the spaghetti squash and carrots in a single layer. Wrap the garlic head in aluminum foil and set on the baking sheet. Spray the squash and carrots with a light coat of cooking spray and roast in the oven until cooked and lightly browned, 30 to 45 minutes.
2. When the vegetables are almost done, in a large pot, heat the oil over medium heat. Add the onions and ginger and cook for about 5 minutes until soft. Add the cumin, oregano, and thyme.
3. Remove the roasted vegetables and garlic from the oven. Squeeze the garlic cloves into the pot and add the roasted carrots and spaghetti squash. Mix together and season with pepper and salt.
4. Add the broth and bring the mixture to a boil. Once boiling, remove from the heat and puree using an immersion blender or placing in a regular blender. Serve immediately and enjoy.
5. Store leftovers in the refrigerator for up to 5 days. To freeze, cool the mixture and pour into a gallon-size resealable freezer bag. Lay it flat in the freezer for up to 3 months.

Per Serving

Calories: **70** | Protein: **0.8g** | Carbs: **11g** | Fiber: **2g** | Fat: **3g** | Sodium: **167mg** | Potassium: **211mg** | Phosphorus: **23mg**

WINTER CHICKEN STEW

Prep time: **20 minutes** | Cook time: **50 minutes** | Serves **6**

- 1 tbsp olive oil
- 1 pound boneless, skinless chicken thighs, cut into 1-inch cubes
- ½ sweet onion, chopped
- 1 tbsp minced garlic
- 2 cups easy chicken stock
- 1 cup plus 2 tbsp water
- 1 carrot, sliced
- 2 celery stalks, sliced
- 1 turnip, sliced thin
- 1 tbsp chopped fresh thyme
- 1 tsp finely chopped fresh rosemary
- 2 tsp cornstarch
- freshly ground black pepper

1. Place a large saucepan on medium-high heat and add the olive oil.
2. Sauté the chicken for about 6 minutes or until it is lightly browned, stirring often.
3. Add the onion and garlic and sauté for 3 minutes.
4. Add the chicken stock, 1 cup water, carrot, celery, and turnip and bring the stew to a boil.
5. Reduce the heat to low and simmer for about 30 minutes or until the chicken is cooked through and tender.
6. Add the thyme and rosemary and simmer for 3 more minutes.
7. In a small bowl, stir together the 2 tbsp water and the cornstarch, and add the mixture to the stew.
8. Stir to incorporate the cornstarch mixture and cook for 3 to 4 minutes or until the stew thickens.
9. Remove from the heat and season with pepper.

Per Serving

Calories: **141** | Fat: **8g** | Carbs: **5g** | Fiber: **5g** | Phosphorus: **53mg** | Potassium: **192mg** | Sodium: **214mg** | Protein: **9g**

CABBAGE STEW

Prep time: 20 minutes | Cook time: 35 minutes | Serves 6

- 1 tsp. unsalted butter
- ½large sweet onion, chopped
- 1 tsp. minced garlic
- 6 cups shredded green cabbage
- 3 celery stalks, chopped with leafy tops
- 1 scallion, both green and white parts, chopped
- 2 tbsps. chopped fresh parsley
- 2 tbsps. freshly squeezed lemon juice
- 1 tbsp. chopped fresh thyme
- 1 tsp. chopped savory
- 1 tsp. chopped fresh oregano
- Water
- 1 cup Fresh green beans, cut into 1-inch pieces
- Ground black pepper

1. Melt the butter in a pot.
2. Sauté the onion and garlic in the melted butter for 3 minutes, or until the vegetables are softened.
3. Add the celery, cabbage, scallion, parsley, lemon juice, thyme, savory, and oregano to the pot, add enough water to cover the vegetables by 4 inches.
4. Bring the soup to a boil. Reduce the heat to low and simmer the soup for 25 minutes or until the vegetables are tender.
5. Season with pepper.

Per Serving

Calories: **33** | Fat: **1g** | Carb: **6g** | Fiber: **2g** | Phosphorus: **29mg** | Potassium: **187mg** | Sodium: **20mg** | Protein: **1g**

HERBED CABBAGE STEW

Prep time: 20 minutes | Cook time: 35 minutes | Serves 6

- 1 tsp unsalted butter
- ½ large sweet onion, chopped
- 1 tsp minced garlic
- 6 cups shredded green cabbage
- 3 celery stalks, chopped with the leafy tops
- 1 scallion, both green and white parts, chopped
- 2 tbsp chopped fresh parsley
- 2 tbsp freshly squeezed lemon juice
- 1 tbsp chopped fresh thyme
- 1 tsp chopped savory
- 1 tsp chopped fresh oregano
- water
- 1 cup fresh green beans, cut into 1-inch pieces
- freshly ground black pepper

1. In a medium stockpot over medium-high heat, melt the butter.
2. Sauté the onion and garlic in the melted butter for about 3 minutes or until the vegetables are softened.
3. Add the cabbage, celery, scallion, parsley, lemon juice, thyme, savory, and oregano to the pot, and add enough water to cover the vegetables by about 4 inches.
4. Bring the soup to a boil, reduce the heat to low, and simmer the soup for about 25 minutes or until the vegetables are tender.
5. Add the green beans and simmer 3 minutes.
6. Season with pepper.

Per Serving

Calories: **33** | Fat: **1g** | Fiber: **3g** | Carbs: **6g** | Phosphorus: **29mg** | Potassium: **187mg** | Sodium: **20mg** | Protein: **1g**

FRENCH ONION SOUP

Prep time: **20 minutes** | Cook time: **50 minutes** | Serves **4**

- 2 tbsp unsalted butter
- 4 vidalia onions, sliced thin
- 2 cups easy chicken stock
- 2 cups water
- 1 tbsp chopped fresh thyme
- freshly ground black pepper

1. In a large saucepan over medium heat, melt the butter.
2. Add the onions to the saucepan and cook them slowly, stirring frequently, for about 30 minutes or until the onions are caramelized and tender.
3. Add the chicken stock and water, and bring the soup to a boil.
4. Reduce the heat to low and simmer the soup for 15 minutes.
5. Stir in the thyme and season the soup with pepper.
6. Serve piping hot.

Per Serving

Calories: **90** | Fat: **6g** | Carbs: **7g** | Fiber: **3g** | Phosphorus: **22mg** | Potassium: **192mg** | Sodium: **57mg** | Protein: **2g**

PAPRIKA PORK SOUP

Prep time: **5 minutes** | Cook time: **35 minutes** | Serves **2**

- 4-ounce sliced pork loin
- 1 tsp black pepper
- 2 minced garlic cloves
- 3 cups water
- 1 tbsp extra-virgin olive oil
- 1 chopped onion
- 1 tbsp paprika

1. Add in the oil, chopped onion and minced garlic.
2. Sauté for 5 minutes on low heat.
3. Add the pork slices to the onions and cook for 7-8 minutes or until browned.
4. Add the water to the pan and bring to a boil on high heat.
5. Reduce heat and simmer for a further 20 minutes or until pork is thoroughly cooked through.
6. Season with pepper to serve.

Per Serving

Calories: **165g** | Protein: **13 g** | Fiber: **5g** | Carbs: **10 g** | Fat: **9 g** | Sodium: **269 mg** | Potassium: **486 mg** | Phosphorus: **158 mg**

CREAMY MUSHROOM SOUP

Prep time: **10 minutes** | Cook time: **15 minutes** | Serves **6**

- 1 lb. mushrooms, sliced
- ½ cup heavy cream
- 4 cups chicken broth
- 1 tbsp. sage, chopped
- ¼ cup butter
- Pepper
- Salt

1. Melt butter in a large pot over medium heat.
2. Add sage and saute for 1 minute.
3. Add mushrooms and cook for 3-5 minutes or until lightly browned.
4. Add broth and stir well and simmer for 5 minutes.
5. Puree the soup using an immersion blender until smooth.
6. Add heavy cream and stir well. Season soup with pepper and salt.
7. Serve hot and enjoy.

Per Serving

Calories: **145** | Fat: **12.5 g** | Carbs: **3.6 g** | Fiber: **3.5g** | Protein: **5.9 g** | Phosphorus: **140mg** | Potassium: **127mg** | Sodium: **75mg**

CURRIED CARROT AND BEET SOUP

Prep time: **10 minutes** | Cook time: **50 minutes** | Serves **4**

- 1 large red beet
- 5 carrots, chopped
- 1 tbsp curry powder
- 3 cups homemade rice milk or unsweetened store-bought rice milk
- freshly ground black pepper
- yogurt, for serving

1. Preheat the oven to 400°F.
2. Wrap the beet in aluminum foil and roast for 45 minutes, until the vegetable is tender when pierced with a fork. Remove from the oven and let cool.
3. In a saucepan, add the carrots and cover with water. Bring to a boil, reduce the heat, cover, and simmer for 10 minutes, until tender.
4. Transfer the carrots and beet to a food processor, and process until smooth. Add the curry powder and rice milk. Season with pepper. Serve topped with a dollop of yogurt.

Per Serving

Calories: **112** | Fat: **1g** | Carbs: **24g** | Fiber: **7g** | Protein: **3g** | Phosphorus: **57mg** | Potassium: **468mg** | Sodium: **129mg**

VIBRANT CARROT SOUP

Prep time: **15 minutes** | Cook time: **25 minutes** | Serves **4**

- 1 tbsp olive oil
- ½ sweet onion, chopped
- 2 tsp grated peeled fresh ginger
- 1 tsp minced fresh garlic
- 4 cups water
- 3 carrots, chopped
- 1 tsp ground turmeric
- ½ cup coconut milk
- 1 tbsp chopped fresh cilantro

1. In a large saucepan over medium-high heat, heat the olive oil.
2. Sauté the onion, ginger, and garlic until softened, about 3 minutes.
3. Stir in the water, carrots, and turmeric. Bring the soup to a boil, reduce the heat to low, and simmer until the carrots are tender, about 20 minutes.
4. Transfer the soup in batches to a food processor (or blender), and process with the coconut milk until the soup is smooth. Return the soup to the pan and reheat.
5. Serve topped with the cilantro.

Per Serving

Calories: **113** | Fat: **10g** | Sodium: **30mg** | Carbs: **7g** | Fiber: **2g** | Phosphorus: **50mg** | Potassium: **200mg** | Protein: **1g**

BEEF AND VEGETABLE SOUP

Prep time: **15 minutes** | Cook time: **55 minutes** | Serves **4**

- 1 pound beef stew
- ½ tsp basil
- 1 cup sliced onions, raw
- 3 ½ cups water
- 1 tsp black pepper
- ½ cup carrots, frozen, diced
- ½ cup green peas, frozen
- ½ cup frozen okra
- ½ cup frozen corn
- ½ tsp thyme

1. Place the black pepper, beef stew, onions, thyme, basil and water in a pot. Cook over medium heat for about 45 minutes.
2. Put in all the frozen vegetables; cook over low heat until the meat is tender. Serve hot.

Per Serving

Calories: **236** | Protein: **12g** | Carbs: **34g** | Fat: **16g** | Fiber: **10g** | Sodium: **136mg** | Potassium: **298mg** | Phosphorus: **174mg**

TURKEY BARLEY STEW

Prep time: **25 minutes** | Cook time: **45 minutes** | Serves **6**

- 1 tsp olive oil
- ½ pound uncooked turkey breast, cut into ½-inch pieces
- ½ sweet onion, chopped
- 1 tsp minced garlic
- 3 cups water
- 1 cup sodium-free chicken stock
- 1 cup shredded green cabbage
- 1 carrot, sliced
- ½ cup barley
- 2 bay leaves
- 2 tbsp fresh parsley leaves
- freshly ground black pepper

1. In a large saucepan over medium-high heat, heat the olive oil. Add the turkey, and sauté until cooked through, about 7 minutes.
2. Add the onion and garlic, and sauté until softened, about 3 minutes.
3. Add the water, stock, cabbage, carrot, barley, and bay leaves. Bring to a boil, then reduce the heat to low, and simmer until the barley and vegetables are tender, about 35 minutes.
4. Remove the bay leaves, and stir in the parsley.
5. Season with pepper, and serve hot.

Per Serving

Calories: **117** | Fat: **1g** | Sodium: **29mg** | Carbs: **15g** | Fiber: **3g** | Phosphorus: **118mg** | Potassium: **200mg** | Protein: **11g**

VEGETABLE LENTIL SOUP

Prep time: **10 minutes** | Cook time: **25 minutes** | Serves **4**

- 1 tbsp extra-virgin olive oil
- ½ sweet onion, diced
- 2 carrots, diced
- 2 celery stalks, diced
- ½ cup lentils
- 5 cups simple chicken broth or low-sodium store-bought chicken stock
- 2 cups sliced chard leaves
- freshly ground black pepper
- juice of 1 lemon

1. In a medium stockpot over medium-high heat, heat the olive oil. Add the onion and stir until softened, about 3 to 5 minutes.
2. Add the carrots, celery, lentils, and broth. Bring to a boil, reduce the heat and simmer, uncovered, for 15 minutes, until the lentils are tender.
3. Add the chard and cook for 3 additional minutes, until wilted.
4. Season with the pepper and lemon juice. Serve.

Per Serving

Calories: **195** | Fat: **6g** | Carbs: **25g** | Fiber: **9g** | Protein: **13g** | Phosphorus: **228mg** | Potassium: **707mg** | Sodium: **157mg**

CHAPTER 11:
DESSERTS

MIXED BERRY PIE

Prep time: **10 minutes** | Cook time: **55 minutes** | Serves **8**

- Pie Crust
- 1½ cups frozen blackberries
- 1 cup frozen blueberries
- 1 cup frozen raspberries
- 1 cup sugar
- ⅓ cup cornstarch
- 1 tbsp ground cinnamon

1. Preheat the oven to 375°F.
2. Combine the blackberries, blueberries, and raspberries in a microwave-safe medium bowl. On low power, thaw the berries in the microwave for 3 to 5 minutes. Watch closely so the berries do not burst. (Alternatively, let the berries thaw on the counter for 20 minutes.)
3. In a small bowl, mix together the sugar, cornstarch, and cinnamon. Add the sugar mixture to the bowl with the thawed berries and mix well.
4. On a floured surface, roll out one round of the pie dough, then transfer it to a 9-inch pie plate. Pour in the berry filling and spread it evenly.
5. Roll out the remaining round of dough and place it over the filling, then pinch the edges together to seal. Cut slits in the top crust. (Alternatively, make a lattice crust by cutting the dough into strips and weaving them in a crosshatch pattern over the filling.)
6. Bake the pie for 45 to 55 minutes, until the crust is golden brown and the juices are bubbling. Let cool on a wire rack for a few minutes before serving.

Per Serving

Calories: **432** | Protein: **4g** | Fat: **16g** | Carbs: **71g** | Fiber: **5g** | Phosphorus: **55mg** | Potassium: **129mg** | Sodium: **3mg**

BLUEBERRY RASPBERRY GALETTE

Prep time: **20 minutes** | Cook time: **30 minutes** | Serves **8**

- 2 cups fresh blueberries
- 1 cup fresh raspberries
- ½ cup sugar
- 1 tbsp cornstarch
- ¼ tsp ground nutmeg
- 1 (9-inch) prepared, flat, unbaked piecrust
- 1 egg, beaten

1. Preheat the oven to 400°F.
2. Line a baking sheet with parchment paper.
3. In a large bowl, add the blueberries, raspberries, sugar, cornstarch, and nutmeg and toss gently to mix together.
4. Lay the piecrust on the parchment paper in the prepared pan, and pour the berry mixture into the center.
5. Spread out the berries, leaving about 1½ inches of bare crust around the edges.
6. Brush the bare crust with the egg. Fold the edges of the crust back over the filling, pressing lightly so the overlapping pastry folds stick together.
7. Bake the galette until the crust is golden and crisp and the berries are bubbling, about 30 minutes.
8. Serve.

Per Serving

Calories: **196** | Fat: **5g** | Sodium: **56mg** | Carbs: **45g** | Fiber: **2g** | Phosphorus: **19mg** | Potassium: **144mg** | Protein: **4g**

STRAWBERRY ICE CREAM

Prep time: **25 minutes** | Cook time: **0 minutes** | Serves **8**

- 1 cup crushed ice
- 1 package frozen strawberries 10-oz (sweetened)
- 1 tbsp lemon juice
- ¾ cup coffee creamer (non-dairy)
- Few drops Red food color
- ½ cup sugar

1. Thaw the strawberries until they break into pieces.
2. In a blender, place all ingredients. Blend until smooth and sugar are dissolved.
3. Pour into a covered bowl. Freeze until firm.

Per Serving

Calories: **198** | Protein: **5g** | Carbs: **27g** | Fat: **18g** | Fiber: **2g** | Sodium: **198mg** | Potassium: **127mg** | Phosphorus: **77mg**

SPICED BAKED APPLE

Prep time: **5 minutes** | Cook time: **10 minutes** | Serves **2 to 4**

- 1 tsp sugar
- 1 brimley apple
- ½ tsp cinnamon

1. Core and place the apple core in a microwave-safe dish.
2. Combine the sugar and spoon the cinnamon and cloves into the center of the apple.
3. Cook for 2 to 3 minutes or until tender, on medium power in the micro. To serve, use a dollop of low-fat cream.

Per Serving

Calories: **148** | Protein: **2g** | Carbs: **42g** | Fat: **2g** | Fiber: **3g** | Sodium: **45mg** | Potassium: **287mg** | Phosphorus: **47mg**

TROPICAL VANILLA SNOW CONE

Prep time: **15 minutes, plus freezing time** | Cook time: **15 minutes** | Serves **4**

- 1 cup canned peaches
- 1 cup pineapple
- 1 cup frozen strawberries
- 6 tbsp water
- 2 tbsp granulated sugar
- 1 tbsp vanilla extract

1. In a large saucepan, mix together the peaches, pineapple, strawberries, water, and sugar over medium-high heat and bring to a boil.
2. Reduce the heat to low and simmer the mixture, stirring occasionally, for 15 minutes.
3. Remove from the heat and let the mixture cool completely, for about 1 hour.
4. Stir in the vanilla and transfer the fruit mixture to a food processor or blender.
5. Purée until smooth, and pour the purée into a 9-by-13-inch glass baking dish.
6. Cover and place the dish in the freezer overnight.
7. When the fruit mixture is completely frozen, use a fork to scrape the sorbet until you have flaked flavored ice.
8. Scoop the ice flakes into 4 serving dishes.

Per Serving

Calories: **92** | Fat: **0g** | Carbs: **22g** | Fiber: **3.5g** | Phosphorus: **17mg** | Potassium: **145mg** | Sodium: **4mg** | Protein: **1g**

CINNAMON APPLE CHIA SEED PUDDING

Prep time: **5 minutes, plus 8 hours to set** | Cook time: **20 minutes** | Serves **2**

- ½ small unpeeled apple, chopped or grated
- ½ cup plain unsweetened almond milk or store-bought
- 2 tbsp chia seeds
- 1 tbsp maple syrup
- ¼ tsp vanilla extract
- ¼ tsp ground cinnamon

1. In a small bowl or 8-ounce mason jar, mix the apple, almond milk, chia seeds, maple syrup, vanilla, and cinnamon.
2. Cover and refrigerate overnight, or for at least 8 hours. When ready to enjoy, stir again.
3. Store in an airtight container in the refrigerator for up to 3 days.

Per Serving

Calories: **210** | Protein: **4g** | Carbs: **34g** | Fiber: **9g** | Fat: **7g** | Sodium: **93mg** | Potassium: **288mg** | Phosphorus: **192mg**

LEMON MOUSSE

Prep time: **10 minutes** | Cook time: **10 minutes** | Serves **4**

- 1 cup coconut cream
- 8 ounces cream cheese, soft
- ¼ cup fresh lemon juice
- 3 pinches salt
- 1 tsp lemon liquid stevia

1. Preheat your oven to 350 °F.
2. Grease a ramekin with butter
3. Beat cream, cream cheese, fresh lemon juice, salt and lemon liquid stevia in a mixer
4. Pour batter into ramekin
5. Bake for 10 minutes, then transfer the mousse to a serving glass
6. Let it chill for 2 hours and serve
7. Enjoy!

Per Serving

Calories: **395** | Fat: **31g** | Carbs: **3g** | Fiber: **5g** | Protein: **5g** | Phosphorus: **80mg** | Potassium: **97mg** | Sodium: **75mg**

CREAM CHEESE POUND CAKE

Prep time: **15 minutes** | Cook time: **1 hour and 45 minutes** | Serves **4 to 6**

- 3 sticks margarine or butter
- 8 ounces cream cheese, softened
- 3 cups of sugar
- 1 ½ tsp vanilla extract
- 4 large eggs
- 4 large egg whites
- 3 cups white cake flour, sifted

1. Preheat a microwave oven to 325 ° F.
2. Until light and smooth, cream the margarine, cream cheese and honey.
3. Add vanilla and beat well.
4. Substitute the egg shells, one at a time and then two at a time with the egg whites, beating well after addition.
5. Mix with the flour. Pour the mixture into a greased and floured muffin tin.
6. Bake for about an hour and a half.
7. Mix and pour the glaze over the cooled cake.

Per Serving

Calories: **301** | Protein: **19g** | Carbs: **87g** | Fat: **16g** | Fiber: **9g** | Sodium: **43mg** | Potassium: **265mg** | Phosphorus: **121mg**

GRAPEFRUIT SORBET

Prep time: **10 minutes** | Cook time: **5 minutes** | Serves **6**

For The Thyme Simple Syrup:

- ½ cup sugar
- ¼ cup water
- 1 fresh thyme sprig

For The Sorbet:

- juice of 6 pink grapefruit
- ¼ cup thyme simple syrup

To Make The Thyme Simple Syrup:

1. In a small saucepan, combine the sugar, water, and thyme. Bring to a boil, turn off the heat, and refrigerate, thyme sprig included, until cold. Strain the thyme sprig from the syrup.

To Make The Sorbet:

1. In a blender, combine the grapefruit juice and ¼ cup of simple syrup, and process.
2. Transfer to an airtight container and freeze for 3 to 4 hours, until firm. Serve.

Per Serving

Calories: **109** | Fat: **0g** | Carbs: **26g** | Fiber: **0g** | Protein: **1g** | Phosphorus: **29mg** | Potassium: **318mg** | Sodium: **2mg**

RAW APPLE CAKE

Prep time: **5 minutes** | Cook time: **1 hour and 10- minutes** | Serves **6**

- ½ c. sugar
- 1 c. shortening
- 2 eggs, beaten
- 2 c. flour
- 2 tsp baking soda
- 2 tsp cinnamon
- 1 tsp cloves
- ¾ c. raisins
- 2 c. chopped apples
- 1 c. sour cream
- 1 c. chopped nuts
- 1 c. cold coffee

1. Grease and flour a 9 x 13 pan.
2. Preheat the oven to 300° F.
3. Mix butter, sugar, beaten eggs, baking soda, flour, cinnamon, raisins, cloves, chopped apples, sour cream, cold coffee and walnuts.
4. Bake for one hour.
5. Cool before serving.

Per Serving

Calories: **301** | Protein: **19g** | Carbs: **87g** | Fat: **16g** | Fiber: **9g** | Sodium: **43mg** | Potassium: **265mg** | Phosphorus: **121mg**

RHUBARB CRUMBLE

Prep time: **15 minutes** | Cook time: **30 minutes** | Serves **6**

- unsalted butter, for greasing the baking dish
- 1 cup all-purpose flour
- ½ cup brown sugar
- ½ tsp ground cinnamon
- ½ cup unsalted butter, at room temperature
- 1 cup chopped rhubarb
- 2 apples, peeled, cored, and sliced thin
- 2 tbsp granulated sugar
- 2 tbsp water

1. Preheat the oven to 325°F.
2. Lightly grease an 8-by-8-inch baking dish with butter; set aside.
3. In a small bowl, stir together the flour, sugar, and cinnamon until well combined.
4. Add the butter and rub the mixture between your fingers until it resembles coarse crumbs.
5. In a medium saucepan, mix together the rhubarb, apple, sugar, and water over medium heat and cook for about 20 minutes or until the rhubarb is soft.
6. Spoon the fruit mixture into the baking dish and evenly top with the crumble.
7. Bake the crumble for 20 to 30 minutes or until golden brown.
8. Serve hot.

Per Serving

Calories: **450** | Fat: **23g** | Carbs: **60g** | Fiber: **5g** | Phosphorus: **51mg** | Potassium: **181mg** | Sodium: **10mg** | Protein: **4g**

PINEAPPLE DELIGHT PIE

Prep time: **10 minutes** | Cook time: **25 minutes** | Serves **4**

- 2 egg whites
- 1 can juice packed pineapple 20-oz (crushed)
- 2/3 cup graham cracker crumbs
- 2 ½ tbsp margarine (melted)
- 1 small package pineapple gelatin (sugar-free)
- 1 tbsp lemon juice
- ¼ tsp cream of tartar

1. In a bowl, mix the cookie crumbs and margarine.
2. Press against an 8" tart pan on the bottom and sides.
3. Bake for 5 minutes at 425°F; cool.
4. In a saucepan, drain the pineapple juice. Drizzle the juice with the gelatin and melt over low heat.
5. Turn off the heat and add the lemon juice and pineapple; cool.
6. Beat egg whites and cream of tartar until they develop stiff peaks.
7. Gently fold in the pineapple mixture. with the help of a spoon, assemble the crust.
8. Chill for several hours.

Per Serving

Calories: **289** | Protein: **14g** | Carbs: **54g** | Fat: **8g** | Fiber: **4g** | Sodium: **235mg** | Potassium: **235mg** | Phosphorus: **118mg**

CHAPTER 12: BROTHS, CONDIMENTS, AND SEASONING MIXES

CURRY GARLIC SEASONING

Prep time: **5 minutes** | Cook time: **20 minutes** | Makes **10 tbsp**

- 4 tbsp dried onion flakes
- 3 tbsp garlic powder
- 1½ tbsp curry powder
- ½ tbsp freshly ground black pepper
- ⅛ tsp ground cayenne pepper

1. In a sealable container, combine the onion flakes, garlic powder, curry powder, black pepper, and cayenne and mix well.
2. This seasoning can be stored at room temperature for up to 1 year. Label and date before storing.

Per Serving

Calories: **21** | Protein: **0.8g** | Carbs: **5g** | Fiber **1g** | Fat: **0g** | Potassium: **83mg** | Phosphorus: **22mg** | Sodium: **2mg**

HOMEMADE MAYONNAISE

Prep time: **10 minutes** | Cook time: **30 minutes** | Makes **1 cup**

- 2 egg yolks, at room temperature
- 1½ tsp freshly squeezed lemon juice
- ¼ tsp mustard powder
- ¾ cup olive oil

1. In a medium bowl, whisk together the yolks, lemon juice, and mustard for about 30 seconds or until well blended.
2. Add the olive oil in a thin, steady stream while whisking for about 3 minutes or until the oil is emulsified and the mayonnaise is thick.
3. Store the mayonnaise in the refrigerator in a sealed container for up to 1 week.

Per Serving

Calories: **97** | Fat: **11g** | Fiber **1g** | Carbs: **0g** | Phosphorus: **9mg** | Potassium: **3mg** | Sodium: **1mg** | Protein: **0g**

SWEET CHILI SAUCE

Prep time: **5 minutes** | Cook time: **5 minutes, plus 30 minutes cooling time** | Makes **¼ cup**

- 2 tbsp water
- ⅛ tsp cornstarch
- 1 small fresh serrano chile, finely chopped
- ¼ cup apple cider vinegar
- ½ cup sugar
- 1 garlic clove, minced
- 1 tsp minced fresh ginger

1. In a small bowl, combine the water and cornstarch to make a paste.
2. In a small saucepan, combine the serrano, vinegar, sugar, garlic, and ginger and bring to a boil. Reduce the heat, stir in the cornstarch paste, and simmer for 2 minutes.
3. Remove from the heat and let cool for 30 minutes at room temperature before serving. Store in an airtight container in the refrigerator for up to 1 month.

Per Serving

Calories: **26** | Protein: **0g** | Fat: **0g** | Carbs: **6g** | Fiber: **0g** | Phosphorus: **1mg** | Potassium: **5mg** | Sodium: **0mg**

CAJUN SEASONING

Prep time: **5 minutes** | Cook time: **30 minutes** | Makes **1¼ cups**

- ½ cup sweet paprika
- ¼ cup garlic powder
- 3 tbsp onion powder
- 3 tbsp freshly ground black pepper
- 2 tbsp dried oregano
- 1 tbsp cayenne pepper
- 1 tbsp dried thyme

1. Put the paprika, garlic powder, onion powder, black pepper, oregano, cayenne pepper, and thyme in a blender, and pulse until the ingredients are ground and well combined.
- Transfer the seasoning mixture to a small container with a lid.
- Store in a cool, dry place for up to 6 months.

Per Serving

Calories: **7** | Fat: **0g** | Carbs: **2g** | Fiber: **1g** | Phosphorus: **8mg** | Potassium: **40mg** | Sodium: **1mg** | Protein: **0g**

HOMEMADE APPLE SAUCE

Prep time: **10 minutes** | Cook time: **25 minutes** | Serves **4**

- 6 lbs peeled apples and cut into 8 slices
- 1 cup apple juice/ apple cider
- 1 lemon juice
- ½ cup brown sugar
- 1 tsp cinnamon powder

1. Combine all ingredients in a saucepan and cook over medium heat for 25 minutes, stirring periodically.
2. In a blender or food processor, carefully puree (do not overfill; divide into two portions if necessary) until smooth.
3. Store in the refrigerator and serve on its own, over ice cream, pork chops, pancakes or wherever you like applesauce.

Per Serving

Calories: **289** | Protein: **8g** | Carbs: **34g** | Fat: **13g** | Fiber: **5g** | Sodium: **76mg** | Potassium: **275mg** | Phosphorus: **189mg**

VEGETABLE BROTH

Prep time: **20 minutes** | Cook time: **25 minutes** | Makes **4 cups**

- 1 tbsp olive oil
- 1 unpeeled onion, sliced
- 2 unpeeled garlic cloves, crushed
- 2 unpeeled carrots, sliced
- 2 celery stalks, cut into 2-inch pieces
- 1 bay leaf
- 1 tsp dried basil leaves
- 5 cups water

1. Heat the olive oil in a large saucepan over medium-high heat.
2. Sauté the onion, garlic, carrot, and celery for 5 minutes, stirring frequently, or until lightly browned.
3. Add the bay leaf, basil, and water to the saucepan and bring to a boil.
4. Reduce the heat to medium-low and simmer for 20 to 22 minutes, stirring occasionally. Skim off and discard any scum that rises to the surface.
5. Strain the stock through a fine-mesh colander into a bowl. Discard the solids.
6. Refrigerate the broth and remove any fat that rises to the top. You can freeze this broth in 1-cup measures to use in recipes.
7. Store in the refrigerator up to 3 days; freeze up to 3 months.

Per Serving

Calories: **31** | Fat: **2g** | Sodium: **21mg** | Potassium: **110mg** | Phosphorus: **14mg** | Carbs: **4g** | Fiber: **1g** | Protein: **0g**

POPPY SEED DRESSING

Prep time: **10 minutes** | Cook time: **10 minutes** | Makes **2 cups**

- ½ cup apple cider or red wine vinegar
- ⅓ cup honey
- ¼ cup freshly squeezed lemon juice
- 1 tbsp Dijon mustard
- 1 cup olive oil
- ½ small sweet onion, minced
- 2 tbsp poppy seeds

1. In a small bowl, whisk together the vinegar, honey, lemon juice, and mustard until well blended.
2. Whisk in the oil, onion, and poppy seeds.
3. Store the dressing in a sealed glass container in the refrigerator for up to 2 weeks.

Per Serving

Calories: **151** | Fat: **14g** | Sodium: **12mg** | Carbs: **7g** | Fiber: **0g** | Phosphorus: **13mg** | Potassium: **30mg** | Protein: **0g**

FIVE INGREDIENT VEGETABLE BROTH

Prep time: **10 minutes** | Cook time: **45 minutes** | Serves **4**

- 1 can chicken broth
- 1 can corn, drained and rinsed
- 1 can refried beans
- 1 can beans, drained and rinsed
- 1 can diced tomatoes

1. In a pot, combine all the ingredients, stirring to mix the refried beans.
2. Cook on low flame, and serve.

Per Serving

Calories: **198** | Protein: **32g** | Carbs: **47g** | Fat: **0g** | Fiber: **2g** | Sodium: **0mg** | Potassium: **55mg** | Phosphorus: **66mg**

MANGO TERIYAKI SAUCE

Prep time: **5 minutes** | Cook time: **25 minutes** | Makes **1¼ cups**

- 3 medjool dates, pitted
- 2 cups water
- ½ cup chopped mango
- 1 tbsp low-sodium soy sauce
- 1 tbsp sesame oil
- 1 tsp rice wine vinegar
- ¼ tsp ground ginger
- ¼ tsp garlic powder

1. In a small bowl, cover the dates with the water and let sit for 15 minutes. Reserve 1 cup of the liquid and drain the dates.
2. In a blender or food processor, combine the dates and reserved water, mango, soy sauce, sesame oil, vinegar, ginger, and garlic powder and puree until smooth.
3. Pour the sauce into a saucepan and bring to a boil over medium heat. Once boiling, remove from the heat and let simmer, stirring occasionally. The sauce should thicken up in 10 to 15 minutes.
4. Store leftovers in an airtight container in the refrigerator for up to 7 days.

Per Serving

Calories: **20** | Protein: **0.2g** | Carbs: **4g** | Fiber **0g** | Fat: **1g** | Sodium: **24mg** | Potassium: **37mg** | Phosphorus: **4mg**

BARBECUE SAUCE

Prep time: **13 minutes** | Cook time: **17 minutes** | Makes **2 cups**

- 1 (14-ounce) can no-salt-added diced tomatoes, with juice
- 1 cup cherry tomatoes, cut in half
- ⅓ cup shredded carrots
- 3 tbsp ketchup
- 2 tbsp freshly squeezed lemon juice
- 1 tbsp honey
- 2 tsp mustard
- 1 tsp paprika
- ½ tsp dried oregano
- ¼ tsp onion powder
- ⅛ tsp cayenne pepper

1. Combine the diced tomatoes, cherry tomatoes, carrots, ketchup, lemon juice, honey, mustard, paprika, oregano, onion powder, and cayenne in a medium saucepan over medium heat and bring to a boil.
2. Reduce the heat to low and simmer for 10 to 12 minutes or until the vegetables are tender.
3. Purée the mixture in a blender or food processor, or right in the saucepan using an immersion blender or a potato masher.
4. Return the mixture to the saucepan if using a blender or food processor. Bring to a simmer again.
5. Simmer the sauce for 5 minutes or until slightly thickened.
6. Cool the sauce for 1 hour in the saucepan, then store in the refrigerator in a container with a lid up to 2 weeks.

Per Serving

Calories: **15** | Fat: **0g** | Sodium: **38mg** | Potassium: **94mg** | Phosphorus: **10mg** | Carbs: **4g** | Fiber: **1g** | Protein: **0g**

CHICKEN STOCK

Prep time: **5 minutes** | Cook time: **25 minutes** | Makes **4 cups**

- 1 tbsp olive oil
- 1 bone-in skin-on chicken breast (3 to 4 ounces)
- pinch salt
- 1 onion, unpeeled, sliced
- 1 carrot, unpeeled, sliced
- 1 bay leaf
- 5 cups water

1. Heat the olive oil in a large saucepan over medium-high heat.
2. Sprinkle the chicken with salt and add to the pan, skin-side down. Brown for 2 minutes.
3. Add the onion and carrot and cook for 1 minute longer.
4. Add the bay leaf and water and bring to a boil.
5. Reduce the heat to medium-low and simmer for 20 to 22 minutes, stirring occasionally. Skim off and discard any scum that rises to the surface.
6. Strain the stock through a fine-mesh colander into a bowl. You can reserve the chicken breast for other recipes, although it may be tough after cooking. Discard the remaining solids.
7. Refrigerate the broth and skim off any fat that rises to the top. You can freeze this stock in 1-cup measures to use in recipes.
8. Store in the refrigerator up to 3 days; freeze up to 3 months.

Per Serving

Calories: **37** | Fat: **2g** | Sodium: **22mg** | Potassium: **85mg** | Phosphorus: **30mg** | Carbs: **2g** | Fiber: **0g** | Protein: **3g**

MEASUREMENT CONVERSION CHART

VOLUME EQUIVALENTS(DRY)

US STANDARD	METRIC (APPROXIMATE)
1/8 teaspoon	0.5 mL
1/4 teaspoon	1 mL
1/2 teaspoon	2 mL
3/4 teaspoon	4 mL
1 teaspoon	5 mL
1 tablespoon	15 mL
1/4 cup	59 mL
1/2 cup	118 mL
3/4 cup	177 mL
1 cup	235 mL
2 cups	475 mL
3 cups	700 mL
4 cups	1 L

VOLUME EQUIVALENTS(LIQUID)

US STANDARD	US STANDARD (OUNCES)	METRIC (APPROXIMATE)
2 tablespoons	1 fl.oz.	30 mL
1/4 cup	2 fl.oz.	60 mL
1/2 cup	4 fl.oz.	120 mL
1 cup	8 fl.oz.	240 mL
1 1/2 cup	12 fl.oz.	355 mL
2 cups or 1 pint	16 fl.oz.	475 mL
4 cups or 1 quart	32 fl.oz.	1 L
1 gallon	128 fl.oz.	4 L

TEMPERATURES EQUIVALENTS

FAHRENHEIT(F)	CELSIUS(C) (APPROXIMATE)
225 °F	107 °C
250 °F	120 °C
275 °F	135 °C
300 °F	150 °C
325 °F	160 °C
350 °F	180 °C
375 °F	190 °C
400 °F	205 °C
425 °F	220 °C
450 °F	235 °C
475 °F	245 °C
500 °F	260 °C

WEIGHT EQUIVALENTS

US STANDARD	METRIC (APPROXIMATE)
1 ounce	28 g
2 ounces	57 g
5 ounces	142 g
10 ounces	284 g
15 ounces	425 g
16 ounces (1 pound)	455 g
1.5 pounds	680 g
2 pounds	907 g

The Dirty Dozen and Clean Fifteen

The Environmental Working Group (EWG) is a nonprofit, nonpartisan organization dedicated to protecting human health and the environment Its mission is to empower people to live healthier lives in a healthier environment. This organization publishes an annual list of the twelve kinds of produce, in sequence, that have the highest amount of pesticide residue-the Dirty Dozen-as well as a list of the fifteen kinds ofproduce that have the least amount of pesticide residue-the Clean Fifteen.

THE DIRTY DOZEN	THE CLEAN FIFTEEN
• The 2016 Dirty Dozen includes the following produce. These are considered among the year's most important produce to buy organic:	• The least critical to buy organically are the Clean Fifteen list. The following are on the 2016 list:

THE DIRTY DOZEN

Strawberries   Spinach
Apples   Tomatoes
Nectarines   Bell peppers
Peaches   Cherry tomatoes
Celery   Cucumbers
Grapes   Kale/collard greens
Cherries   Hot peppers

THE CLEAN FIFTEEN

Avocados   Papayas
Corn   Kiw
Pineapples   Eggplant
Cabbage   Honeydew
Sweet peas   Grapefruit
Onions   Cantaloupe
Asparagus   Cauliflower
Mangos

• *The Dirty Dozen list contains two additional itemskale/collard greens and hot peppers-because they tend to contain trace levels of highly hazardous pesticides.*

• *Some of the sweet corn sold in the United States are made from genetically engineered (GE) seedstock. Buy organic varieties of these crops to avoid GE produce.*

APPENDIX 3: INDEX

Hey there!

Wow, can you believe we've reached the end of this culinary journey together? I'm truly thrilled and filled with joy as I think back on all the recipes we've shared and the flavors we've discovered. This experience, blending a bit of tradition with our own unique twists, has been a journey of love for good food. And knowing you've been out there, giving these dishes a try, has made this adventure incredibly special to me.

Even though we're turning the last page of this book, I hope our conversation about all things delicious doesn't have to end. I cherish your thoughts, your experiments, and yes, even those moments when things didn't go as planned. Every piece of feedback you share is invaluable, helping to enrich this experience for us all.

I'd be so grateful if you could take a moment to share your thoughts with me, be it through a review on Amazon or any other place you feel comfortable expressing yourself online. Whether it's praise, constructive criticism, or even an idea for how we might do things differently in the future, your input is what truly makes this journey meaningful.

This book is a piece of my heart, offered to you with all the love and enthusiasm I have for cooking. But it's your engagement and your words that elevate it to something truly extraordinary.

Thank you from the bottom of my heart for being such an integral part of this culinary adventure. Your openness to trying new things and sharing your experiences has been the greatest gift.

Catch you later,

Renee R. Legere

Printed in Great Britain
by Amazon

47703145R30046